# FRODO & HARRY

# FRODO & HARRY

## Understanding Visual Media and Its Impact on Our Lives

## TED BAEHR & TOM SNYDER

CROSSWAY BOOKS

A DIVISION OF
GOOD NEWS PUBLISHERS
WHEATON, ILLINOIS

*Frodo & Harry*

Copyright © 2003 by Ted Baehr & Tom Snyder

Published by Crossway Books
a division of Good News Publishers
1300 Crescent Street
Wheaton, Illinois 60187

Cover design: Josh Dennis

First printing 2003

Printed in the United States of America

ISBN 1-58134-559-3

The author is represented by Alive Communications, Inc., 7680 Goddard Street, Suite 200, Colorado Springs, CO 80920.

---

**Library of Congress Cataloging-in-Publication Data**
Baehr, Theodore.
    Frodo and Harry : Understanding Visual Media and Its Impact on Our
Lives / by Ted Baehr and Tom Snyder.
        p.  cm.
    Includes bibliographical references.
    ISBN 1-58134-559-3 (tpb. : alk. paper)
    1. Tolkien, J. R. R. (John Ronald Reuel), 1892-1973. Lord of the rings.
2. Tolkien, J. R. R. (John Ronald Reuel), 1892-1973—Religion.  3. Fantasy
fiction, English—Religious aspects—Christianity.  4. Fantasy fiction,
English—History and criticism.  5. Rowling, J. K.—Characters—Harry
Potter.  6. Baggins, Frodo (Fictitious character).  7. Potter, Harry (Fictitious
character)  8. Christianity and literature.  9. Rowling, J. K.—Religion.
I. Snyder, Thomas Lee, 1952-    . II. Title.
PR6039.O32L6324      2003
823'.912—dc21                                               2003014668

| BP |    | 13 | 12 | 11 | 10 | 09 | 08 | 07 | 06 | 05 | 04 | 03 |
|----|----|----|----|----|----|----|----|----|----|----|----|----|
| 15 | 14 | 13 | 12 | 11 | 10 | 9  | 8  | 7  | 6  | 5  | 4  | 3  | 2 | 1 |

With love and great
thanksgiving:

Dr. Ted Baehr dedicates this book
to our Lord and Savior Jesus Christ
and to Lili, Peirce, Jim, Robby, and Evy.

Dr. Tom Snyder dedicates this book
to his wife, Jan, and his parents, Tom and Vivian.

Also we want to thank Marvin Padgett, Lane Dennis,
Chip MacGregor, Beverly Hartz, directors,
supporters, and friends.

*"If anyone causes one of these little ones
who believe in me to sin,
it would be better for him to have a large millstone
hung around his neck
and to be drowned in the depths of the sea."*
MATTHEW 18:6 (NIV)


Father in heaven,
Thank you for giving us the Good News of new life
available to each of us through your Son, Jesus the Christ.
Thank you for giving us your Holy Spirit, our Teacher.
Bless all who read this book.
Grant us, as your people, wisdom, knowledge,
and understanding.
Help us to reveal your Word to those in need.
Help us to lift up your holy name, Jesus, through the power
of your Holy Spirit.
AMEN

# CONTENTS

# PREFACE:
## DIVINE ENCOUNTERS AND PARABLES

*A good story is a journey toward God. It reminds us of
the Master Storyteller. A good story is a holy thing.*
BEVERLY HARTZ, CHAPLAIN,
MISSION HOSPITAL

One day more than seventy years ago, two literary giants in England stood talking about language, stories, and religion. In the middle of the conversation, the taller gentleman blurted to his slightly balding companion, "Here's my point: Just as a word is an invention about an object or an idea, so a story can be an invention about Truth."

"I've loved stories since I was a boy," the other man admitted. "Especially stories about heroism and sacrifice, death, and resurrection. . . . But when it comes to Christianity . . . well, that's another matter. I simply don't understand how the life and death of Someone Else (whoever he was) 2,000 years ago can help me here and now."

The first man earnestly replied, "But don't you see, Jack? The Christian story is the greatest story of them all. Because it's the *real* story. The historical event that fulfills the tales and shows us what they mean."

About a week later, Jack—also known as C. S. Lewis, the author of the classic books *Mere Christianity* and The Chronicles of Narnia (among many other works)—announced his conversion to Christianity to a friend. Lewis attributed his decision largely to his conversation with J. R. R. Tolkien.[1]

Of course, Tolkien is the author of one of the greatest works of the twentieth century, The Lord of the Rings, which has been transformed into a magnificent movie trilogy by director Peter Jackson. Although Tolkien, a Roman Catholic, didn't always see eye to eye with Lewis, who was more inclined toward Protestantism, they both understood the truth of the ultimate story.

## STORYTELLING AND MYTHMAKING

As Tolkien and Lewis said so long ago, stories matter deeply. They connect us to our personal history and to the history of all time and culture. From the moment when we hear our mother or father say to us as a child, "Once upon a time," we are meaning seekers and meaning makers. We strive to connect ourselves to our experiences and the experiences of others. We are addicted to those "aha!" moments in our lives when we see meaning, purpose, and significance.

Stories help us do this. They bring us laughter, tears, and joy. They stimulate our minds and stir our imaginations. Stories help us escape our daily lives for a while and visit different times, places, and people. They can arouse our compassion and empathy, spur us toward truth and love, or sometimes even incite us toward hatred or violence.

Different kinds of stories satisfy different needs. For example, a comedy evokes a different response from us than a tragedy. A hard news story on page 1 affects us differently than a human interest story in the magazine section or a celebrity profile next to the movie or television listings. While stories meet different needs, many stories share common themes, settings, character types, situations, and other recurrent archetypal patterns. They may even possess a timeless universal quality.

Many stories focus on one individual, a heroic figure who overcomes many trials and tribulations to defeat evil or to attain a valuable goal. We identify with such heroes because we recognize that we are each on our own journey or quest. How a hero's journey informs and illuminates our own journey is significant. We look for answers in stories.

However, every story has a worldview, a way of viewing reality, truth, the universe, the human condition, and the supernatural world. Looking carefully at a story, we can examine the motifs, meanings, values, and principles that it suggests. For example, a story can have a redemptive Christian worldview that shows people their need for salvation through a personal faith in the gospel of Jesus Christ, or it can have a secular humanist worldview that explicitly or implicitly attacks Christianity. By examining a story's worldview, we can determine the cultural ideals and the moral, philosophical, social, psychological, spiritual, and aesthetic messages that the story conveys, as well as determine the emotions the story evokes.

The book you have in your hands, *Frodo and Harry: Understanding Visual Media and Its Impact on Our Lives*, will look at two stories that have battled for supremacy at the movie box office, in bookstores, and in the hearts and minds of people throughout the world. The movie versions of the first two books in each of these series are the top four moneymakers in the last four years worldwide, earning more than four billion dollars overall! Clearly, a lot of children, a lot of teenagers, and many parents have seen these movies and read these books.

It has been said that the shortest distance between truth and a human being is a story. The purpose of this book is to examine the worldview of these two stories and determine how well each travels the distance toward truth. Second, we will explore many aspects of how to look at the media, to discern the good from the bad, using these two stories as case studies. In the process, you will gain the practical tools you need to evaluate the impact that these cultural icons, and others like them, may have on your children and grandchildren. We hope that this book will enable you to develop an entertainment strategy for your family that will help rather than hinder their walk with God.

# ◆PART◆
# ONE

# I

# IT'S ONLY A MOVIE . . . AND OTHER STAR WARS

*If we educate a man's mind but not his heart, we have an educated barbarian.*

THEODORE ROOSEVELT

Once upon a time, our grandparents taught their children that they could talk about anything at the dinner table except religion, sex, and politics. These were topics that aroused deeply felt personal opinions and often impolite conversation. These days it seems that sexual preferences or religious notions hardly raise an eyebrow. Now if you want to get embroiled in a truly controversial subject, start talking about your favorite movie!

Perhaps this heightened sense of the importance of movies and the desire to defend one's position on a particular movie is good to a degree, because it shows that people understand the power of films. As the great bard William Shakespeare noted, the "pen is mightier than the sword." Fast forward 500 years from Shakespeare's time, and we see that the twenty-first century entertainment mass media is mightier than the six-teenth-century printed word, though much of the mass media of enter-tainment starts with the written word.

So it is not surprising that the level of heated discussion, particularly in the Christian and conservative community, increased tremendously with the release of the first Harry Potter movie and intensified with the release of the first episode of the Lord of the Rings trilogy soon thereafter. In fact, the polarization of opinion became so heated that people were calling names and putting out false information.

## HELP IS ON ITS WAY

Imagine, if you will, your child coming home one day and informing you that the teacher is reading one of the Harry Potter books to her class. You have heard stories about these books in your church; so you go to the teacher and ask her to excuse your child from the Harry Potter readings. She refuses, saying that the readings are an essential part of your child's reading lessons and help keep the students engaged during the lessons.

You go to the principal to complain, but the principal tells you that she must protect the teacher's academic freedom. Besides, what are you—some kind of censor from the religious right?

So you go to the school board and voice your complaints, along with one or two other parents, but the school board members don't seem much interested because most of the other people in the district, including the leaders in the local teachers union affiliated with the National Education Association, are apathetic about your concerns. So you might suggest that in the interest of equal time, the children might also read the most popular book of all time—the Bible. But then the double standard comes into play, and everyone tells you that there must be a separation of church and state.

Chagrined, you go back to your home and wonder if perhaps all of these people are right. Perhaps you *are* being a bit overprotective and shrill. Besides, you don't want to be an old fuddy-duddy censor telling other people what to read, think, watch, and hear. It's only a children's book, after all, and your child can read lots of other books that would be safer and more wholesome.

If you are one of those parents struggling with what position to take on Harry Potter, be encouraged. Help is on its way to you and your child. This book will enable you to unravel the debate about Harry Potter and about Lord of the Rings so that you can help your child and others become media wise. Most believers and people of faith and values will welcome this discussion since God's Word tells us to seek wisdom, knowledge, and understanding.

Although this book is aimed at Christian parents, Christian educators of children, teenagers, and young adults, and any believer who takes the Word of God seriously, others will also benefit from the insights and principles proffered. Our book is not as comprehensive as we might like. Therefore, if you think an important point is left out of the discussion, we would welcome further dialogue. Contact us at www.movieguide.org.

Our purpose is to help people of faith and values see and understand the difference between the two movies that have been adapted from the popular literary works. Today's movie audiences need the tools not only to exercise discernment but also to make wise choices. This book will contrast the fictional "real world" of the Lord of the Rings with the "occult world" of Harry Potter. We will help the audience ask the right questions about these films.

In addition, we need to ask: Should we interpret a movie by reading our own opinions into the work in question, or should we let the work speak for itself? This book will shed light on these questions, as well as help audiences understand the nature of fantasy, myth, genre, and the various different critical tools necessary to develop an informed judgment about art and entertainment. Considering the influence that the characters of Frodo and Harry have had on our culture, this book will be an extremely important and helpful tool for families, home schools, Christian schools, and churches.

## WITCHCRAFT AND THE INQUISITION

On the surface, much of the debate about Harry Potter revolves around the issue of witchcraft. One side dismisses any concerns about the witchcraft in Harry Potter as an archaic inquisitorial attitude, while the other cringes at the thought that millions of young children might be tempted to become witches and warlocks.

C. S. Lewis observed that people can make two opposite but equally wrongheaded mistakes about the devil—taking him too seriously or not taking him seriously enough. One of these extremes ignores the supernatural world, and the other undervalues the victory of Jesus Christ on the cross over the devil and his minions.

God clearly condemns the practice of witchcraft in his Word (as in

Deuteronomy 18:10 KJV: "There shall not be found among you *any one* that maketh his son or his daughter to pass through the fire, *or* that useth divination, *or* an observer of times, or an enchanter, or a witch"; or 1 Samuel 15:23 KJV: "For rebellion *is as* the sin of witchcraft, and stubbornness *is as* iniquity and idolatry"). It is understandable that people whose worldviews are not rooted in the Bible would scoff at any concerns about witchcraft, since they do not know God's teachings on this subject. It is surprising, however, when people who identify themselves as believing Christians do not take a stand against the witchcraft in Harry Potter. This failure tends to confuse those who are not theologically astute.

Some who expressed concerns about Harry Potter focused on the Old Testament verses that condemned witchcraft. They assumed that both believing Jews and Christians considered the Old Testament or Hebrew Scripture to be the authentic Word of God. However, they seemed unaware that, after rejecting Jesus Christ as the Messiah, a significant part of Judaism embraced astrology, occultism, and other pagan beliefs. Many Jewish leaders understood that the Hebrew Testament clearly pointed to Jesus as the Messiah. So they needed to reinterpret their Scriptures and their faith to exclude that possibility. Their reliance on the Talmud and then later on the Kabbalah, rather than the Hebrew Scriptures, was to a degree an outgrowth of this rejection of the Messiah.

Christians sometimes dismiss the Bible's denunciation of witchcraft and sorcery as only applying to the Jews. In fact, God's abhorrence and condemnation of witchcraft extends throughout the Bible and includes the apostles' condemnation of Simon the Magician in the book of Acts and culminates in the clear words of Revelation 21:8 (KJV): "But the fearful, and unbelieving, and the abominable, and murderers, and whoremongers, and sorcerers, and idolaters, and all liars, shall have their part in the lake which burneth with fire and brimstone: which is the second death"; and, 22:15 (KJV): "Outside are the dogs and sorcerers and the sexually immoral and murderers and idolaters, and everyone who loves and practices falsehood."

One of the problems with the application of these verses today is a lack of theological understanding about how to read Scripture. The key is to reclaim those analytical tools the church used for centuries. To understand Scripture, the reader needs to let the clear meaning of the text speak for itself (exegesis), rather than reading our opinions back into the text (eisegesis). Moreover, the text should always be read in context, and Scripture should be used to interpret Scripture. Finally, the application of a biblical principle or the analysis of an issue should proceed from Scripture to the tradition of the church to the application of informed reason—never the other way around. Too often in today's world, contemporary opinions trump tradition and Scripture. To read and apply Scripture requires analytical tools and standards.

In our so-called postmodern (or neo-pagan) age, this analytical approach may require some reflection to comprehend its value. Theology is the knowledge of God, and God's Word calls us to know him so that we can make him known. Therefore, every Christian is a theologian to some degree. Acquiring and developing the mental tools to know him and his will better should be the goal of everyone who loves him.

Even so, as we seek to understand the debate over Harry Potter and Lord of the Rings, we must keep in mind that we are saved by grace and that the Good News of Jesus Christ redeems us in the midst of our insufficiency.

## THE GROUND OF BEING

During the height of the debate over Harry Potter and Lord of the Rings, I (Ted) went to tea with a Malaysian woman who was attending an evangelical Christian school. She said there was a great debate at her school about Harry Potter and Lord of the Rings. Caught in an area of the world where tribalism, paganism, Islam, Christianity, and Hinduism are competing for attention, this woman came to an understanding of the difference between these two movies after only a brief explanation of ontology.

Ontology refers to the ground of being, the very essence or nature of the world in which we live. To Hindus and many occultists, we live in an imaginary world, a Great Thought, an Illusion. To a Marxist, we live in a materialistic world. To a Christian, we live in a real world with real pain, real suffering, a real God, and a real salvation.

Harry Potter films and books say that the world can be manipulated through magic. Things change shape, nothing is really real. For a

Christian, however, things are real, and, as shown in Lord of the Rings, if you are mortally wounded in a sword fight, you can die. Thus, your actions have consequences.

## WHAT DIFFERENCE DOES IT MAKE?

It makes a world of difference. Mother Teresa saw the poor and dying on the streets of Calcutta as real people. So she started picking them off the streets and taking care of them. The Hindus saw them as just part of Maya, or the World of Illusion. Hindus were so offended by her care of the poor that they tried to kill her. Materialists, of course, would say that the poor and dying are just fodder—let them die. The ultimate goal of a materialist would be to get rid of all religion and just become a disinterested scientist.

The good news, however, is that the Creator, who created the reality, is ready to rescue us from our fallenness through the gospel of Jesus Christ. In a Christian world, life has meaning. Since it was designed by a good God, life has hope. Rescued by God through Jesus Christ's sacrificial death, we are safe to build a family and a civilization.

Actually both C. S. Lewis and Tolkien have been guilty of creating confusion in Christians' minds about magic. These men were part of a writer's group, the Inklings, that tried to reinvest the word *magic* with mythic Christian meaning. In The Chronicles of Narnia, Lewis uses magic as a synonym for laws that God has written into the universe. Although the stories by Lewis and Tolkien are fantasy, they should not be confused with the world of the occult. The worlds Lewis and Tolkien created are based on reality with real consequences and real hope.

One of the reasons the debate is raging is that many Christians have drifted away from a solid understanding of the Bible's Trinitarian theology and have become apathetic or lukewarm about biblical truth. Instead, they have adapted or adopted all sorts of unbiblical doctrines, corrupting their theology, clouding their minds, and chaining their hearts. That's why the battle for people's souls, or the battle between good and evil, is really a battle for biblical truth. This is a battle that you and your family must win.

Everyone has a worldview or theology concerning the Bible. Even those who deny that the Bible is God's inerrant Word or deny that it is true are proclaiming a particular worldview and theology about the Bible, its truth, and its applicability to human affairs.

Ultimately, there can be no real neutrality concerning God, the Bible, truth, Jesus Christ, the nature of being (or ontology), good and evil, etc. We are all responsible for the worldviews and attitudes we take. The question is, how should we decide what to believe? By what authority? By what standard?

As Paul tells Timothy in 2 Timothy 3:10-17, the Bible is the highest authority, the great standard that, when read and studied, points us toward right thinking and thoroughly equips us "for every good work." The Bible convinces us and convicts us. As such, it shows us beyond a shadow of a doubt that it is far better to be like Mother Teresa or C. S. Lewis than a Hindu worshiping cows or an Eskimo cowering in his igloo for fear of offending some demon. And though we may be ridiculed by "evil people" who "go on from bad to worse, deceiving and being deceived" (2 Tim. 3:13), we can know with certainty that nothing "will be able to separate us from the love of God in Christ Jesus our Lord" (Rom. 8:39). That is the ground of difference between the Christian and the non-Christian.

# II

# SOMETHING ABOUT HARRY

*Blessed is the man who walks not in the counsel of the wicked, nor stands in the way of sinners, nor sits in the seat of scoffers.*

PSALM 1:1

A lot of hype surrounds the Harry Potter books and movies. In some ways the hype is deserved because the books have sold millions of copies, and the first two movies have made more than $1.5 billion at the box office worldwide, plus hundreds of millions more at the video store. Even so, parents and children need to know the dangers this cultural phenomenon poses.

While it is important to know if there is any gratuitous foul language, violence, sex, nudity, and drug use in a movie or television program, the ultimate value of the work is determined by its premise and worldview. It is these factors—which include its philosophy, theology, and morality—that make the work true, false, heretical, or evil. Each work represents the personal vision of the creator and creators behind it. This vision will express the worldview that the creator has decided, consciously or unconsciously, to represent in the work.

A worldview is a way of interpreting reality. Everyone has a worldview. Every worldview has a way of defining the nature of being or existence; a way of looking at the physical universe and how it came to be a theology or doctrine of God and man's relationship to God; a view the human soul and the mental, emotional, spiritual, and interior life; a view of human beings and their environment and culture; a philosophy of values, especially moral values. Finally, although everyone has a worldview, that worldview may be confused, mixed, or underdeveloped. This seems to be the case with many people.

So what is the premise and the worldview of the Harry Potter books and movies? How will the premise and worldview in these tales of heroic fantasy affect people with impressionable minds or confused or undeveloped worldviews?

## PLOTS

The story of the first book and movie, *Harry Potter and the Sorcerer's Stone* (known as *Harry Potter and the Philosopher's Stone* in England, which is a more accurate title), begins with little Harry Potter's parents being killed by the evil wizard Voldemort. This wizard tries to put a powerful curse on baby Harry but fails because the baby apparently has some powerful natural magic of his own. Voldemort disappears, and Professor Dumbledore (played by Richard Harris), the headmaster of Hogwarts School of Witchcraft and Wizardry, drops the baby at the house of Harry's nonmagical aunt and uncle, Petunia and Vernon Dursley.

Ten years later, after being teased and abused by the Dursleys and their obnoxious, fat son Dudley, Harry receives a special invitation to attend Hogwarts School of Witchcraft and Wizardry. Mr. Dursley tries to stop Harry from going, but the big, hairy groundskeeper from Hogwarts, Hagrid (played marvelously by Robbie Coltrane), takes Harry away. Hagrid introduces Harry to the goblin bank where his parents kept their money. Harry gets some money and some school supplies. Then he's off to Platform Nine and Three-Quarters to catch the train that will take him to Hogwarts. Before Harry goes, however, Hagrid takes a mysterious, small package out of one of the goblin vaults.

At Hogwarts Harry becomes friends with two other first-year students, Ron and Hermione. They are all assigned to the same house, Gryffindor, one of four dormitories that will compete for the House Cup based on points. The three children undergo a series of adventures, not the least of which is an encounter with a twelve-foot troll. They disobey orders and find themselves exploring various parts of the labyrinthine Hogwarts School. Meanwhile, Harry finds he has an aptitude for quidditch, which is sort of a rugby-style soccer game played on flying broomsticks. During Harry's first match, it looks as if one of the teachers at the school, the dark, mysterious Professor Snape, tries to knock Harry off his broomstick, a plot that Hermione foils.

Eventually Harry, Hermione, and Ron discover where Hagrid and Professor Dumbledore have hidden the mysterious package from the goblin bank. It turns out to be the infamous sorcerer's stone, whose spell brings immortality and converts items into gold. This stone is just what the evil Voldemort needs to bring himself back to life in another body. Harry and his two friends suspect that Professor Snape is trying to steal the stone. When Dumbledore is suspiciously called away to London, Harry and his two friends try to get the stone before Snape does.

The production values in *Harry Potter and the Sorcerer's Stone* are excellent and state of the art. The movie almost perfectly depicts the fantasy elements from the book. The set designs in this movie are visual treats. The special effects are also terrific, especially the twelve-foot-troll that invades the school and the exciting quidditch game.

The three young actors portraying Harry, Ron, and Hermione do a wonderful job. Daniel Radcliffe fits the role of Harry like a glove. Director Chris Columbus creatively uses the boy's subtle ability to express emotions, which keeps viewers interested. Emma Watson as Hermione and Rupert Grint as Ron are also delightful. Among the adult actors, Richard Harris, Maggie Smith, John Hurt, and Alan Rickman—playing Dumbledore, Professor McGonagall, Mr. Ollivander, and Professor Snape, respectively—are particularly noteworthy.

The production problems with the movie are virtually the same problems with the book. Despite the care with which the fantasy elements and the characters are handled, the book and the movie have little sense of plotting. There are several digressions in the middle of the story, which take away from the plot involving Harry, the villain Voldemort, and the sorcerer's stone. The story finally gets back on track toward the end, but by then it's almost worn out its welcome. The film also suffers in that we see so little of the main villain, Voldemort, though there is a lot of talk about him.

The second filmed edition of Harry Potter, *Harry Potter and the*

*Chamber of Secrets*, is slightly better constructed and more emotionally involving than the first movie. However, knowledge of the Harry Potter books or the first movie is helpful for fully comprehending this second in the series. It is not a stand-alone movie.

Like the first two books and the first movie, *Chamber of Secrets* suffers from an ambling, prolonged introduction that doesn't quite clarify what the jeopardy is or who the villain is. With nothing at stake, the movie at first appears to be a series of vignettes. When the jeopardy does engage, the movie becomes an exciting action-adventure fantasy that follows the classic model of heroic tales, but then it has several curtain call endings. Several of these manipulate the audience into feeling good about the characters in the movie and perhaps even clapping for the movie.

*Harry Potter and the Chamber of Secrets* opens with Harry back at home with his horrible uncle, weak aunt, and miserable cousin Dudley. These caricature people make it clear that they do not like Harry and that he should stay in his room and not interfere with their lives. Back in Harry's room, a nicely animated CGI (computer-generated imagery) house elf named Dobby appears, who is one of the few real characters in the movie. He warns Harry not to go back to Hogwarts School of Witchcraft and Wizardry. When Harry refuses, Dobby makes a racket and turns a party for Uncle Vernon's boss into a disaster. Of course, Harry gets blamed. Uncle Vernon decides to put bars on the window to Harry's room, but three of Harry's friends from Hogwarts, including the red-haired Ron Weasley and his brothers, rescue Harry from the clutches of his Muggle relatives in an old British car that can fly.

After several adventures, Ron and Harry make their way back to Hogwarts and find out that some strange things are happening at the school, all of which point to a curse that will be unleashed if the ancient Chamber of Secrets is opened. Harry finds a book with no writing that speaks to him and tells him about a boy named Tom Riddle, who found the Chamber of Secrets fifty years before. One by one, several people are turned to stone. Harry unlocks the Chamber of Secrets riddle and ends up in mortal combat with a monstrous snake and the person behind the plot. After this, there are several curtain calls, which tie up loose ends in the story and promote great feelings about each one of the previously harmed or incapacitated characters.

*Harry Potter and the Chamber of Secrets* did well at the box office and at the video store. Although there are some plot holes, loose ends, and dramatic flaws, the movie has enough vim, vigor, and melodramatic moments to make it very popular. The film also has an intriguing mystery and climactic ending, and the actors are enjoyable to watch, especially Kenneth Branagh as an incompetent, conceited sorcerer.

## SOME PROS AND CONS

With its grab bag of myth conceptions, allegory, and illusions, the movie has elements that could be used to present Christian truth. For example, Dumbledore calls Harry to make a wise choice, the Chamber of Secrets lies beneath a baptismal font, snakes and those who command them are seen as the source of evil, and the story contains a strong sense of self-sacrifice for the benefit of others. Furthermore, there are elements of good triumphing over evil. These are just a few of the many spiritually redemptive and incarnational moments. They follow the redemptive pattern of heroic tales where the hero descends into a dark underworld to do battle with the forces of evil and returns victorious to the world above, where he presents a boon of some kind to those who have been oppressed. These elements can be used for evangelism, which will please those who want to like the movie and those who want to claim that the film has some Christian merit.

Morally, however, *Harry Potter and the Chamber of Secrets*, like the other books and movies, has some problems. At the end Dumbledore tells Harry that he's broken at least half a dozen school rules, but then awards him the school's highest award. In the first movie the children not only break school rules, but they lie about it. Furthermore, that story gives a wink and a nod at the fact that no one can keep a secret among the witches and wizards because of all the gossip. Looking at the series as a whole, readers and viewers find Harry blackmailing his uncle, using trickery and deception, lying to get out of trouble, and seeking revenge on his student enemies.

The Harry Potter worldview teaches a kind of moral relativism. Disobeying rules, practicing witchcraft, consulting the spirits of dead people, and lying are all treated as praiseworthy, especially if they are successful.

Anyone who has studied the influence of television and film on children will realize that these behaviors will send a clear message to children in the imaginative stage of development. Since Harry is an attractive and well-meaning hero, this role modeling is even more powerful. Are these the messages you want to teach your children?

Also disturbing from a moral perspective in *Chamber* is a suggestion of infanticide when the mandrakes are taken screaming from their pots, and the students are told that they will kill the mandrakes to produce an antidote to cure the petrifaction of the people. Thus the book and the movie have a subtext that is abhorrent to the God of the Bible, who views all human life as precious, whether fully formed, partially formed, or handicapped.

On the other hand, both the book and the movie contain a clear refutation of racism and of an incipient National Socialist/fascist group of wizards who want to wipe out all mixed-blood wizards. Here is a constructive theme, similar to those in all of the stories in the series. For example, in *Sorcerer's Stone* are themes of love and sacrifice, rejection of false immortality, and a warning about not getting lost in false dreams and desires.

## DABBLING IN THE OCCULT

All of the Harry Potter books and movies are certainly spiritual but not in a way that conforms to Christian or Jewish theology and a biblical worldview. They are deeply rooted in the occult. Novelist Michael D. O'Brien pinpoints specific practices:

> Student witches and wizards are taught to use their wands to cast hexes and spells to alter their environments, punish small foes, and defend themselves against more sinister enemies. Transfiguration lessons show them how to change objects and people into other kinds of creatures—sometimes against their will. In Potions class they make brews that can be used to control others.[1]

Occult practices are not just minor occurrences in Harry Potter. They pervade the whole series. Witchcraft, even when couched in a humorous fantasy realm, is rebellion against God and the order he has established. In Harry Potter the heroes all practice witchcraft to defeat the villains. These heroes have become role models for millions of children around the world.

Harry Potter's pagan, occult worldview portrays the evil witches and warlocks as having tremendous power and says that the heroes can only succeed by participating in occult and often secret activity. There is no transcendent, sovereign person or principle controlling the use of this occult power. It is a power with no ultimate authority behind it.

The premise that drives most of the plots in Harry Potter reflects this anti-Christian worldview. Thus, in the stories the more powerful and more attractive wizard, Harry, defeats the less powerful, less attractive one, Lord Voldemort.

Anthropologically and psychologically speaking, Harry Potter's worldview contrasts two different worlds—the mundane, cruel, ignorant world of the nonmagical people with the magical, adventurous, secret, dangerous world represented by Hogwarts School of Witchcraft and Wizardry. Harry is caught between these two worlds, but his ultimate goal is to leave the mundane world behind for the world of witchcraft.

Later in the series, however, Harry learns that living in the mundane world helps protect him from Lord Voldemort and his minions. He also learns that witchcraft enables him to have more control over his life in the mundane world. In this way, the Harry Potter books and movies teach children that using witchcraft and other occult powers can help them overcome obstacles in their own lives and improve their mental, emotional, and spiritual lives.

Harry Potter's pagan worldview also presents an occult view of existence and the physical universe. The story is filled with magical thinking and sets forth a nominalistic universe in which the physical world is but an illusion. God's laws are suspended or absent. Thus, Harry and his friends manipulate reality to defeat or humiliate their enemies and sometimes even play funny tricks on people. Their supernatural abilities reflect a godless universe with few redemptive aspects. This view contrasts strongly with the Christian, moral worldview in Lord of the Rings, which contains many profound Christian metaphors. Harry Potter is not just a harmless fantasy. It is a dangerous fantasy filled with false pagan idols in a world thirsting for spiritual fulfillment.

Make no mistake, God condemns witchcraft regardless of how

sweet and subtle it is. Moses gives the Hebrews God's personal instructions: "Let no one be found among you who sacrifices his son or daughter in the fire, who practices divination or sorcery, interprets omens, engages in witchcraft, or casts spells, or who is a medium or spiritist or who consults the dead" (Deut. 18:10-11 NIV).

Although there may be some differences between the kind of witchcraft, sorcery, divination, and spell-casting in Harry Potter, which is a work of fantasy fiction, and the practices listed in this biblical passage, the words have the same basic range of meaning. In fact, this biblical passage is one of the clearest passages in Scripture. Muddying the waters by fudging on the meanings of the words in the passage would be very dangerous and foolish; yet that is what many defenders of Harry Potter mistakenly do.

But there's a larger problem here, as Michael O'Brien points out:

> While Rowling posits the "good" use of occult powers against their misuse, thus imparting to her sub-creation an apparent aura of morality, the cumulative effect is to shift our understanding of the battle lines between good and evil. The border is never defined. Of course, the archetype of "misuse" is Voldemort, whose savage cruelty and will to power is blatantly evil, yet the reader is lulled into minimizing or forgetting altogether that Harry himself, and many other of the "good" characters, frequently use the same powers on a lesser scale, supposedly for good ends. The false notion of "the end justifies the means" is the subtext throughout. The author's characterization and plot continually reinforce the message that if a person is "nice," if he means well, is brave and loyal to his friends, he can pretty much do as he sees fit to combat horrific evil—magic powers being the ideal weapon. This is consistent with the author's confused notions of authority. In reality, magic is an attempt to bypass the limitations of human nature and the authority of God, in order to obtain power over material creation and the will of others through manipulation of the supernatural. Magic is about taking control. It is a fundamental rejection of the divine order in creation. In the first book of Samuel (15:23) divination is equated with the spirit of rebellion. . . .
>
> With occult themes now a part of mainstream culture, the Potter series is juxtaposed between a growing amount of blatantly diabolical material for the young on one hand, and on the other a tide of cultural material that redefines good and evil in subtler ways. Thus, it appears

as a healthier specimen of what has been more or less normalized all around us. . . . Our society is saturated in the false notion that a lesser evil (in this case, "good sorcery") is preferable to the great evil of Satanism, a message further reinforced by the books' condemnation of the extremes of diabolical behavior. What we so often forget is that the "lesser evil" concept is a classic adversarial tactic in the great war between good and evil—the real war in which we are all immersed. The evil spirits seek to attract us to evil behavior by first offering us evil thoughts disguised as good. In opposition to these, they set up great evils from which we naturally recoil, and offer the lesser evils as the antidote. If the lesser evil is presented with a little window-dressing of virtue or morality (or the modern term "values"), we can turn to it assuming we are making a choice for a good. . . .

. . . [T]hese novels seem at first glance to reject evil by dissociating magic from the diabolic. Yet in the real world they are always associated. We must ask ourselves if they really can be separated without negative consequences. If magic is presented as a good, or as morally neutral, is there not an increased likelihood that when a young person encounters opportunities to explore the world of real magic he will be less able to resist its attractions?[2]

## GNOSTICISM

In addition to glamorizing and neutralizing something evil, the Potter books and movies resurrect ideas from an ancient philosophy that once seriously challenged the Christian faith. That philosophy is gnosticism.

The term *gnosticism* comes from the Greek word for knowledge, *gnosis*. In a religious or spiritual context, *gnosis* refers to secret religious or spiritual knowledge. Gnosticism is a heretical system of belief that began in the second century, about 100 years after the death and resurrection of Jesus Christ. This system envisions two equally powerful worlds at war, a world of light and a world of darkness. Within this dualistic view of reality, "two superhuman forces (the good god of light and the demons of darkness), and . . . two parts of human beings (a good soul imprisoned in an evil body)"[3] are engaged in an apocalyptic struggle. Human beings contain sparks of the divine god of light, but they must become conscious of this fact through a special, mystical, secret knowledge, or *gnosis*, so they can attain salvation and redemption from the evil material world and return to the god of light.

One gnostic story talks about a redeemer sent by the god of light to waken the human souls to their divine essence. This gnostic redeemer gives the human souls a secret knowledge about their divinity and shows them the way to defeat evil and return to the nonmaterial world of light. The redeemer then goes back to the heavenly realm "to prepare the way for his followers after their death."[4]

Many, if not most, of the gnostic believers in the second century applied this gnostic redeemer story to Jesus Christ and his teachings. The story is false, heretical, and unhistorical, however, for several reasons. First, it denies the New Testament's teaching on the physical incarnation and resurrection of Jesus Christ, the only begotten Son of God. These historical events had many reliable, credible eyewitnesses, as shown by the documents in the New Testament and information from other early extra-biblical historical sources. Secondly, gnosticism undermines the existence and power of God's physical creation in order to create a nonmaterial ultimate reality with special, magical power. Thirdly, it denies the redemption of the physical world through the gospel of Jesus Christ. Finally, it denies the fundamental distinction between God and his creation, including the distinction between God and man, that exists in the basic teachings of the biblical text. This last denial is especially prevalent in New Age versions of gnosticism, where the New Age believer is asked to "wake up" to the "Christ consciousness" or "Buddha consciousness" within so that he or she can become one with God. Instead, the Christian concept of God offers the power of the indwelling Holy Spirit to transform us, as we yield to that power, into Christlikeness. We have communion with God, but we are not gods, nor do we become gods.

As Father Alfonso Aguilar notes in "Into the Gnostic Wonderland," in the April 6-12, 2003, issue of the *National Catholic Register*, the Harry Potter books and movies portray the battle between the "good" magic practiced by Harry and his witchcraft friends versus the "dark arts" practiced by the Dark Lord Voldemort and his followers. During the stories, Harry Potter becomes more and more aware that he is a wizard and that he has amazing powers. Thus in contrast to Frodo and his hobbit companions in Lord of the Rings who become more conscious that they have a destiny to play in something greater than themselves, Harry Potter becomes conscious of the "spark" within that makes him special. In this way, the Harry Potter books and movies display an elitism that you don't find in the humble attitudes of the small hobbits in The Lord of the Rings trilogy. The form of elitism in the Potter stories values most those who are best at doing magic. They possess secret, esoteric knowledge that gives them power over others—a primary tenet of gnosticism.

The nascent gnosticism in Harry Potter is an important part of its occult, pagan worldview. Harry's immersion in the secret world of occultism and witchcraft leads to increasingly intense confrontations with his nemesis, the evil Lord Voldemort, and Voldemort's evil minions. The dark arts practiced by the villains are not seen as a negation of the good, but as a mirror reflection. It is a dualistic, gnostic view of good and evil that contradicts what our children are learning from us and our church. The immense popularity of this gnostic presentation presents a very real challenge to both churches and families.

Gnosticism teaches that reality can be manipulated by the enlightened person who has secret knowledge of the divine spark within himself. In contrast, the Judeo-Christian tradition acknowledges a world that contains real pain, real suffering, and the real need for a real savior, though Jews and Christians today differ on who that savior is. In *Chamber of Secrets*, witches and warlocks can create substantial things (food, spells, and monsters) out of nothing. The world is not real, but merely a great thought, and the key to manipulating that reality is merely saying the right words in the right way at the right time. Thus those with superior or gnostic knowledge and power can become the sorcerers or witches who determine reality. In effect, they can become as gods. This, of course, violates basic truths in the biblical worldview of both Judaism and Christianity, just as does the opposite extreme—that everything is material and doesn't matter.

It is interesting to note that the story in *Chamber of Secrets* involves a book that has the power to destroy. Thus the movie has the same problematic potential as the book in the story that causes all the trouble. At some level, therefore, the author of the Harry Potter books realizes that some books do indeed have the power to destroy.

In this respect millions of young children may not rush out and start practicing witchcraft, a practice that both the Hebrew Scriptures and the New Testament condemn. But even so, the occult, New Age, gnostic worldview of the books and movies and their moral relativism will lead millions of children away from Christ and into nonbiblical or even anti-biblical teachings that will certainly destroy these children, as well as the societies in which they live.

Whoever controls the media does indeed control the culture. Not everyone has a strong theology or ideology, but the culture will be dominated by one theology and ideology or another sooner or later. You must decide, therefore, whether you want your culture and your family to be dominated by biblical Christianity, which gives people the freedom to worship as they wish and yet allows the church to freely evangelize people in love and in truth, or by something like the ideas in Harry Potter and other contemporary books and movies, or, worse, by a pagan theology and ideology like that of Nazi Germany where millions were slaughtered in the name of a mad, godless dictator.

## AN ATTACK ON BIBLICAL CHRISTIANITY?

J. K. Rowling, the creator and author of the Harry Potter books, and her defenders have expressed surprise that many committed Christians have objected to and even shunned the Harry Potter works because of the occult witchcraft depicted in them, such as casting spells, mixing potions, using wands, and divination.

Why should these protests against the Harry Potter series surprise them? After all, in Rowling's own writing, the witches and wizards at Hogwarts School of Witchcraft and Wizardry complain about the non-magical people in the "real" world who reject the use of witchcraft and magic or who express contempt, prejudice, and/or hatred for those who practice these arts. In fact, the books and the movies based on the books depict the Dursleys—Harry Potter's uncle, aunt, and cousin—as the worst kind of prejudiced anti-witchcraft bigots possible. In effect, Rowling and her defenders have poisoned the well in advance against any Christians who might object to the occult witchcraft described in the book.

Just imagine for a moment a child who reads the Harry Potter books and watches the movies saying to his teachers and peers, "Oh, those Christians who hate Harry Potter are just like Uncle Dursley—rude, hateful, and obnoxious!" The books and movies teach children and teenagers, and adults for that matter, to mock and hate the Bible-believing Christians who object to the Harry Potter witchcraft mania.

To prove this point, consider the passage in Rowling's third book, *Harry Potter and the Prisoner of Azkaban*, where Harry has to secretly do his witchcraft and reads a passage from Bathilda Bagshot's *A History of Magic*. Harry reads:

> Nonmagic people (more commonly known as Muggles) were particularly afraid of magic in medieval times, but not very good at recognizing it. On the rare occasion that they did catch a real witch or wizard, burning had no effect whatsoever. The witch or wizard would perform a basic Flame Freezing Charm and then pretend to shriek with pain while enjoying a gentle, tickling sensation. Indeed, Wendelin the Weird enjoyed being burned so much that she allowed herself to be caught no less than forty-seven times in various disguises.[5]

This passage is intended to be funny, and it is. It also, however, is highly offensive for several reasons, and it shows the disingenuous nature of many of the arguments of Rowling's defenders.

First, the passage shows that, despite the attack on prejudice and bigotry in the second book and movie, *Harry Potter and the Chamber of Secrets*, Rowling and her witchcraft heroes continue to use a derogatory, bigoted, hateful term—Muggle—for those people who are born with no magical power. In fact, according to the tenth edition of *Merriam-Webster's Collegiate Dictionary*, the term *mug* is also a British word for a fool, a blockhead, or a person who is easily deceived. So to the witches and warlocks at Hogwarts, the Muggles are a bunch of fools and blockheads, a group of people who are easily deceived and gullible.

The passage from *Prisoner of Azkaban* mocks the nonmagical people for wanting to rid their society of the use of "magic," which, in the context of the Harry Potter books and movies and their occult worldview, is really a euphemism for witchcraft and sorcery. The passage from the fictional book that Harry reads says that the Muggles in "medieval times" were "particularly afraid" of witchcraft, but that they were so clueless that they often didn't recognize the use of it. Because of the stupidity and gullibility of the Muggles in medieval times, the witches and "wizards," or sorcerers, who actually got caught were still able to use their special powers and witchcraft to fake their deaths when they were burned at the stake. So nonmagical people (or Christians) who want to demonize and stamp out witchcraft have an irrational fear or "phobia" of witchcraft, but they are so stupid and gullible that a witch can easily fool these blockheads. Also, according to the passage, the nonmagical people in medieval times were particularly irrational or phobic, stupid, and gullible because they were not as "smart" as modern people.

Nothing could be further from the truth, however. The Middle Ages was a time of great Christian expansion in Europe. Although the period had its share of horrors, the same is true of today's world. In fact, within the last 100 years, Hitler was sending millions of innocent people to the gas chambers, and Joseph Stalin was murdering millions more. Furthermore, slavery is still going on in some parts of the world today, and the wars, terrorism, and persecutions of dictators like Saddam Hussein and madmen like Osama bin Laden are still a vivid memory for many. In fact, it could even be argued that in the twentieth and twenty-first centuries, modern, secular, "post-Christian" society is far more barbaric than the Christian kingdoms populating Europe during the Middle Ages.

As cultural historian Christopher Dawson notes in his classic text, *Religion and the Rise of Western Culture*, Christianity had an incredibly powerful and positive *civilizing* effect on the barbarian cultures in the British Isles, Western Europe, Eastern Europe, and Eurasia. For example, Christianity played an important part in preserving and establishing moral and civil laws; protecting the integrity of the family; creating medieval universities that serve as the direct ancestors of modern ones; preserving ancient literature; limiting, controlling, and eventually eliminating the horrors of slavery; and sowing the seeds of separation between sectarian ecclesiastical hierarchies and political governments. "It was only by Christianity and the elements of a higher culture transmitted to them by the Church," writes Dawson, "that Western Europe acquired unity and form."[6]

Dawson goes on to tell how this Christian culture extended its influence toward Eastern Europe and the Russian peoples. Christianity, he adds, "was not concerned with the life of nature or with culture as a part of the order of nature, but with the redemption and regeneration of humanity by the Incarnation of the Divine Word."[7] The influence of Christian culture transformed and regenerated barbarian culture and "by degrees the woody swamp became a hermitage, a religious house, a farm, and abbey, a village, a seminary, a school of learning and a city."[8]

Other fair-minded scholars agree with Dawson's description of the positive impact of Christianity on the medieval societies that grew out of the collapse of the Roman Empire. Walter Burkert, for example, writes that Christianity established strong religious communities that had many positive impacts, such as "a concern for the poor, economic cooperation quite uncommon in pagan religion, and the inclusion of the family as the basic unity of piety in the religious system."[9] Spiritual and moral education of children by parents became more important, Burkert adds, and the practice of exposing handicapped children to the deadly elements of nature was outlawed. Historian Earle E. Cairns adds, "The moral tone was improved by the mitigation of the evils of slavery, the elevation of the position of women, and the softening of the horrors of feudal war. The Roman church sponsored what relief and charitable work was done in the Middle Ages. It provided an intellectual synthesis for life in the theological system that the Scholastics developed and it impressed on men their solidarity as members of the church."[10]

Of course, as the Bible proclaims in Genesis 8:6, "the intentions of man's heart are evil from his youth," and the new Christian culture in Europe and Eurasia did not create perfect human societies or utopias. However, as the new feudal kingdoms grew in power, and as new medieval universities began to sprout, the power of God's transcendent truth, justice, goodness, love, and beauty began to spread to many nations.

Moreover, although Rowling's comments on the Middle Ages mention the practice of burning witches at the stake, the fact is that most of the witch burnings were confined to Switzerland, Germany, and France between 1550 and 1650—times of social turmoil. About 25 percent of the victims were male, and most of them were executed by community courts, not church authorities. It is also important to note that some, if not many, of these victims were also accused of using witchcraft to kill people deliberately. Even so, Numbers 35:31 in the Hebrew Scriptures section of the Christian Bible points out that under God's law an automatic death penalty is only reserved for first-degree murder. Death penalties for all other capital crimes in God's law could be ameliorated by a "ransom"—a fine and a payment of restitution to the allegedly injured parties. Also, the amount of the ransom had to fit the crime. The victim couldn't, for instance, force the convicted criminal to pay for the loss of both eyes when only one eye was lost. That, by the way, is the real meaning behind the famous phrase, "an eye for an eye and a tooth for a tooth."

What is the implicit intent of this passage and of Harry Potter's mockery of those who shun the practice of witchcraft in all its forms? It appears to be a subtle but unambiguous and politically-correct attack on biblical Christianity and Bible-believing Christians. By creating characters like the Dursleys and passages like the one in *Prisoner of Azkaban*, J. K. Rowling implicitly attacks and mocks the attitudes and beliefs of millions of Christians who accept the traditional moral standards of the Bible. Her defenders let her get away with it by 1) creating superficial and even false descriptions of the pagan, occult worldview that dominates the Harry Potter series, which tries to appeal to the masses by stealing some moral and redemptive elements from Christianity, and 2) minimizing the negative impacts that such abhorrent, malignant worldviews, philosophies, theologies, and ideologies can have on children, teenagers, and adults.

In effect, the defenders of Harry Potter are saying to the Christians who oppose them, "What are you silly, gullible, stupid, ignorant, hateful people so upset about here?" Discerning people will dismiss the Potterites' politically-correct notions and fanciful arguments for what they actually are—superficial, hypocritical rationalizations made from a standpoint that ultimately ignores the truth, justice, power, goodness, and beauty of the Word of God.

## PATTERNS OF BELIEF

The fourth book in the Harry Potter series, *The Goblet of Fire*, increases the stakes in the series, but it takes a long time to get there. The 734-page book climaxes in a major confrontation between Harry and the evil Lord Voldemort, who is finally able to resurrect his human body through a magic potion. Despite its gruesome aspects, the scene is the most emotional moment in the whole series, because it focuses on the victims Voldemort has murdered, including a new friend of Harry's and Harry's parents. A duel between Harry and Lord Voldemort, featuring their two magical wands, conjures up the spirits of these victims, which deftly increases the emotional effect of the duel on Harry and on the reader.

Although the fourth book extols positive moral values such as bravery and fairness, the moral outlook is mixed. For instance, cheating is considered normal in the Triwizard Tournament that takes up most of the story; practical jokes and curses against one's enemies, and sometimes even one's friends, are considered charming and humorous; Harry and his friends continue to lie occasionally to teachers and break school rules; and the underage students are allowed to drink a low-alcohol beverage called butterbeer. Another aspect that discerning readers may notice is the high level of secrecy in the books, not only among the bad witches and sorcerers, but even among the good witches and sorcerers. Harry and his friends Ron and Hermione keep secrets from the "good" teachers in the book, but "good" witches and sorcerers like Professor Dumbledore have their own secret plots. Keeping the witchcraft world secret from the nonmagical human beings is another major element in the Harry Potter series.

In the real world, this need for secrecy symbolizes one of the worst elements of witchcraft and other occult practices, which the Bible considers sinful and evil. Witchcraft covens rely on secret rituals and ceremonies, frequently occurring at night, which only a chosen few may attend. In fact, the very word *occult* means something dark or evil that is hidden.

*Harry Potter and the Goblet of Fire* also shows the nominalistic, pagan worldview that occult practices generate. For example, at one point in this book, Harry participates in a classroom session where the students practice fighting off a magical curse from the teacher. Harry almost defeats the curse by using his willpower. This is an important scene because it promotes the nominalistic view that physical and supernatural reality can be manipulated simply by using the power of one's mind. "Mind over matter" nominalism is a major teaching of such heretical and non-Christian or anti-Christian philosophies as Christian Science, Hinduism, Buddhism, and the New Age. Nominalism devalues God's creation because it describes the nature of the physical realm as an illusion. Nominalism also can lead to the heresy of gnosticism, which holds that Christ's resurrection was not a physical resurrection but only a spiritual one. In reality, however, Christ's resurrection not only redeems the spiritual side of humanity; it also redeems the physical world. Unfortunately, many liberal Christian theologians and churches, and even some more conservative ones, have bought into the heretical lies of nominalism and gnosticism. That may even be why the Harry Potter craze does not bother some of these Christians.

Christian philosopher and Tolkien scholar Richard Purtill notes that Tolkien made a distinction between what he called "primary belief" and "secondary belief."[11] Primary belief is what believers give to a religious text like the Gospel of Matthew in the New Testament. Secondary belief is the kind of belief readers give to a work of fiction like *Harry Potter and the Goblet of Fire* or The Lord of the Rings. Using Tolkien's terminology, we might be able to see why some people don't think the Harry Potter books present a problem for the young, impressionable reader. After all, these books are supposed to be fantasy, not reality. The Harry Potter defenders would say that it's silly, if not downright stupid, to treat the books as if they were real treatises on witchcraft and other occult practices.

Purtill, however, makes another distinction about belief. He notes something called "intermediate belief," the belief that the pre-Christian world gave to things like the myths about the Greek and Roman gods or Homer's *Iliad*. In these stories the Greek gods take active roles in the war between Greece and Troy.[12] Intermediate belief, according to Purtill, lies somewhere between primary and secondary belief. Some liberal theologians and scholars have intermediate belief in the New Testament stories of Jesus Christ, which they think contain some elements of historical fact and truth but are not completely factual or true.

As the scientific literature cited later in this book strongly indicates, many children and teenagers in particular stages of cognitive or psychological development, and even some adults, may not be able to completely distinguish between reality and fantasy, or between primary, secondary, and intermediate belief when they read a book like *Harry Potter and the Goblet of Fire* or the latest book, *Harry Potter and the Order of the Phoenix*. That is why you may see some children acting out the occult and pagan practices depicted in the media even though these are fictional. It is also why nineteen-year-old Josh Cooke of Virginia allegedly became obsessed with *The Matrix* movies and brutally gunned down his own mother and father.[13]

Of course, some Christians have accused Tolkien's Lord of the Rings of having the same negative influence. For instance, the popular Dungeons and Dragons role-playing game was developed out of a love of Tolkien's book. This game, created by Gary Gygax and Dave Arneson, usually features characters who do magical spells resembling the kind of spells that real witches and sorcerers try to do. Dungeons and Dragons and its direct descendents, such as Advanced Dungeons and Dragons, have indeed enticed many young people to engage in witchcraft, sorcery, and paganism in real life. However, these games have been created without the Christian worldview and anti-sorcery themes explicit in Tolkien's story. What began as a love for the world created by Tolkien in Lord of the Rings has become a pagan fascination with occultism, fantasy, and non-Christian mythology. The Dungeons and Dragons games do not encourage players to create partially-developed, much less fully-developed, Christian characters who fight evil with goodness in the spirit of Jesus Christ and his followers.

In the same way as Dungeons and Dragons perhaps, the Harry Potter books use the fantasy genre developed by Tolkien and add a dangerous layer of non-Christian beliefs, sentiments, and practices that draw many children, teenagers, and adults away from the one true God. The goal of Christians should be to reclaim the Harry Potter fans and lead them to Jesus Christ, not to encourage their fanaticism.

Another possible negative result of Tolkien's work is the influence of Lord of the Rings on the radical environmentalist movement. In the story, Tolkien takes a dim view of the industrialization that the evil "wizard" Saruman brings to the peaceful Shire of the hobbits. In reality Tolkien was disturbed by the modern factories, highways, and vehicles that polluted the bucolic landscape of his beloved English countryside. Tolkien's environmentalism, however, stopped short of the worshipful attitude that many radical environmentalists take toward nature. Many of them venerate animals, trees, and plants above the lives of people.

In actuality The Lord of the Rings book contains passages where parts of nature have turned just as dangerous and evil as Saruman's destruction of nature. As Bradley J. Birzer notes in *J. R. R. Tolkien's Sanctifying Myth: Understanding Middle-Earth*, the mechanized trench warfare that Tolkien witnessed firsthand during World War I gave him a horror of the dangers of mechanization, modernization, and big government. He thought these forces endangered small towns, villages, rural areas, and the wonders of nature. This attitude, however, did not result in a worship of creation instead of the Creator, says Birzer. In fact, in *The Fellowship of the Ring* and in *The Silmarillion*, Tolkien reveals that Radagast, one of three angelic messengers sent to elves and men from the archangels watching over the earth, has become so enamored of nature that the evil Saruman is able to deceive him. Thus, the message of Tolkien in these works is the same message as the Bible: Nature is a gift from God, and man is supposed to "act as its steward,"[14] not as its destroyer, but we must not worship nature or value it more highly than human life.

## HEROES AND ROLE MODELS

In the Harry Potter books and movies, Harry and his two heroic friends, Ron and Hermione, triumph over the villains by using their own means. Among the methods they use are, no doubt, bravery, intelligence, and perseverance, but they also use witchcraft, lies, and break school rules— three things for which they are ultimately rewarded.

In the Lord of the Rings trilogy and first two movies, however, Frodo and his companions triumph because of the unseen hand of God. They reflect the essential Christian worldview of the original author, J. R. R. Tolkien. For example, Frodo asks Gandalf why the evil magical ring has come to him. Gandalf replies that he thinks Frodo was meant to have the ring. Later Frodo tells Gandalf that maybe they should kill the evil Gollum creature, a former hobbit who was corrupted by the wicked power of the ring and now wants to get it back. Gandalf replies that perhaps there is another purpose in keeping Gollum alive. "Many that live deserve death," Gandalf says. "And some that die deserve life. Can you give it to them? Then do not be too eager to deal out death in judgment."[15] Gandalf's implicit reference to God moves Frodo to show mercy to Gollum, who eventually plays an important role in the positive resolution of the battle against evil in the trilogy. So Gandalf, one of God's angelic delegates on Middle Earth, conveys redemptive insights to Frodo on the grace and mercy that ultimately save Middle Earth from the powers of darkness.

Michael O'Brien contrasts Tolkien's use of magic with Rowling's:

> Supernatural powers, Tolkien demonstrates repeatedly, are very much a domain infested by the "deceits of the Enemy," used for domination of other creatures' free will. As such they are metaphors of sin and spiritual bondage. By contrast, Gandalf's very limited use of preternatural powers is never used to overwhelm, deceive or defile. . . .
>
> Much of the neopagan use of magic is the converse of this. . . . In the Harry Potter series, for example, Harry resists and eventually overcomes Voldemort with the very powers the Dark Lord himself uses. Harry is the reverse image of Frodo. Rowling portrays his victory over evil as the fruit of esoteric knowledge and power. This is Gnosticism. Tolkien portrays Frodo's victory over evil as the fruit of humility, obedience and courage in a state of radical suffering. This is Christianity. Harry's world is about pride, Frodo's about sacrificial love. There is, of course, plenty of courage and love in the Harry Potter series, but it is this very mixing of truth and untruth which makes it so deceptive. Courage and love can be found in all peoples, even those involved in the worst forms of paganism. The presence of such virtues does not automatically justify an error-filled work of fiction. In Potter-world the characters are engaged in activities which in real life corrupt us, weaken the will, darken the mind, and pull the practitioner down into spiritual bondage. Rowling's characters go deeper and deeper into that world without displaying any negative side effects, only an increase in "character." This is a lie. Moreover, it is the Satanic lie which deceived us in Eden: You can have knowledge of good and evil, you can have Godly powers, and you will not die, you will not even be harmed by it—you will have enhanced life.[16]

Another important difference between these two works is that The Lord of the Rings is an epic story that takes place in a mythic fantasy realm where supernatural forces are in conflict. The evil supernatural forces are led by a shadowy demon who appears only as a large yellow eye. Although these demonic forces put the earthly realms of the men, hobbits, dwarves, and elves at grave risk, there is still good in the world because the supernatural world outside these earthly realms is ruled by more powerful spiritual forces, which are ultimately controlled by God, who is called Ilúvatar or Eru in Tolkien's mythology.

The Harry Potter books and movies take place at a school for witchcraft and wizardry where good and evil witches and sorcerers use the supernatural powers of the occult to battle for power and where the secret witchcraft world sometimes comes into conflict with the outside world of the nonmagic folk. Their struggle is not really a moral battle except in the sense that Harry and his friends are protecting the world of witchcraft from the racist witches and sorcerers who want to destroy all Muggles and all witches and sorcerers who do not have pure blood.

Not only are the worldviews completely different in the design of both sagas, their view of heroism is also different, and the worlds or environments in which they take place are different. These are important differences even though the two sagas may share other qualities that seem, at least on the surface, to be the same.

## CONCLUSION

Unlike The Lord of the Rings, the Harry Potter books and movies reflect a pagan, gnostic, and occult worldview. Their worldview is ultimately irrational and elitist and does not reflect the real world where real actions have real consequences. Furthermore, it contradicts the philosophy, theology, worldview, and ideology of Christianity and violates the laws of God, which clearly condemn the type of occult witchcraft used by Harry and the other characters. Finally, though the Harry Potter stories are entertaining and contain some redemptive, moral elements, these positive qualities are undermined by the poor role models depicted in the stories.

Despite protestations to the contrary, these negative elements in Harry Potter can have a negative effect on children, teenagers, and adults. Many scientific studies, cited later in this book, show that this is indeed the case. Parents and churches, therefore, need to know the dangers that this popular cultural phenomenon poses so that they can protect their children, grandchildren, and future generations.

If, however, children and teenagers do see the Harry Potter movies, and many will, remind them that Jesus Christ is always ready to liberate them from fear and witchcraft if they call on his name. Help them think through the various elements of the movie. Here are a few media-wise questions you can ask them:

1. Is it good that Harry is rewarded for breaking the rules?
2. Would you want your friends or enemies to be able to cast spells on you?

3. Would you want to live in a world where reality changes frequently (stairs move, passageways disappear, animals change into goblets)?

4. Would you want to live in a world where other people could change your reality?

5. How is Harry a hero? What makes him a hero? Is he a good role model?

6. Do heroes disobey the rules? If so, when and why?

7. Who is the villain? Why?

8. Does the movie honor God or the Bible? Why or why not?

9. Why does the movie include an image of a Christmas tree with a star on top? What does this image mean?

10. Were parts of the movie scary to you? Why or why not? Is it good to be scared?

11. Hagrid asks Harry if he ever made anything happen when he was angry or scared, and Harry made his cousin fall into the snake pit when he was angry at him. Should we hurt others or take revenge on them even if they deserve it? Would we want others to hurt us or take revenge on us in secret using magic?

12. What is the purpose of magic and witchcraft?

13. Should we try to use secret power over others or over our environment? Should someone else try to use secret powers on us?

14. Why is witchcraft selfish?

15. The serpent in the Garden of Eden, who is Satan, asked Eve if she wanted to be as God. Would you like to be as God? Do you ever make mistakes? Are you smart enough and wise enough not to make mistakes?

16. Would you want others to be as God, such as those who could hurt you?

17. What would it be like in a world where everyone had supernatural powers to manipulate other people in secret?

18. Would you really like to live at Hogwarts? Why?

19. Would you like to ride a broomstick? What if you fell off at a great height?

20. Would you like to have everything in your home or school always shifting around and changing so you never knew your way to your room?

21. Would you like to meet Fluffy, the ghosts, or any of the scary creatures in the movie? What would you do if you met them? What if you couldn't remember the right spell or say the words right or wave the wand properly? Do you ever make mistakes? What if you made a mistake when in the presence of bad creatures or evil people?

22. Magic seems to fail at times. Harry's parents, as powerful and skillful as they were, were killed by another witch. Would you like to know about a power that never fails and never makes mistakes?

23. When the occult magic fails, what does a witch or wizard do? To whom can they turn? Who's ultimately in charge?

24. Would you like to know about a greater supernatural power that is always good and always loves you?

25. Would you like to live in a world where the better witch wins all the battles even if that witch was not you?

26. Would you like to live in a world where good may not triumph?

27. Would you like to live in a world created by a good God who loves you and would never hurt you and who wants to save you from all the bad people and things in the world?

# III

# THE RING OF
# TRUTH

*In all these things we are more than conquerors through
him who loved us.*

ROMANS 8:37 (NIV)

Tolkien's Lord of the Rings trilogy and the background mythology
to his work, published by his son Christopher, have not been
immune to spirited attacks from the Christian community. The claim is
that The Lord of the Rings has a pagan worldview that, like Harry
Potter, is full of occult magic and mythical creatures. Some critics even
go so far as to claim that Tolkien's works teach human reincarnation.

Is any of this true?

## DIVINE MYTHOLOGY

The Lord of the Rings is an epic story taking place in a mythic fantasy
realm called Middle Earth in a mythic past, where supernatural forces
are in conflict. In the story a wandering "wizard" named Gandalf visits
the pastoral land of the hobbits, a race of pint-sized human-like creatures. Gandalf convinces an elderly hobbit named Bilbo to hand down
a mysterious magical ring to his young ward, Frodo.

Years later (in the book version), Gandalf learns the truth behind
the magical ring. It is an evil ring forged secretly by an evil being known
as Sauron the Great, the Dark Lord. With the ring, which can tempt and
enslave lesser beings who use it, Sauron can control nineteen other mag-

ical rings. Seven of these rings were owned by the lords of dwarves, a race of miners; nine of them were owned by nine human kings whom Sauron has subdued; three of the rings have been hidden by the elves, a special created race of tall human-like beings whom God has made immortal and who can never die a natural death. Sauron lost the Ring of Power long, long ago in a battle with the elven kings and Isildur, the former King of Men, but now his spirit has learned that the ring still exists. His minions are searching all of Middle Earth to get it back for him; so Gandalf convinces Frodo to leave the hobbit lands, known as the Shire, and take the Ring of Power to the elven kingdom city of Rivendell.

Eventually Gandalf, Frodo, Frodo's three hobbit companions, a mysterious man called Aragorn, a man called Boromir from the kingdom of Gondor, a dwarf named Gimli, and an elf named Legolas form a fellowship in Rivendell. The fellowship's goal is to take the ring to the volcano mountain called Mount Doom, deep in the heart of Sauron's kingdom of Mordor. Only the volcano fires of Mount Doom can destroy the ring and end Sauron's threat to Middle Earth.

The rest of The Lord of the Rings describes a series of fantastic adventures, including many perilous battles and wondrous encounters with mythical creatures. The trilogy is a moving, exciting tale of courage, loyalty, humility, mercy, and sacrifice. Many have called Lord of the Rings the best novel written in the twentieth century.

The Silmarillion, published about six years after Tolkien's death, presents the mythological background to the story. A lengthy series of appendices at the end of The Lord of the Rings, however, gives some hints of that background. The appendices also tell what happens to the characters in the story after the main adventures described in the story. In The Silmarillion readers learn that Gandalf is not really a wizard at all but a lesser angel who serves nine archangels who watch over the world under the authority of God, who is called Eru, or "The One," and is sometimes called Ilúvatar, or "Father of All."[1] Sauron is another angel, but a demonic one who has sided with the satanic figure in The Silmarillion, a powerful archangel called Melkor or Morgoth, "the Black Enemy." Morgoth is eventually subdued, but Sauron lives on until he is subsequently destroyed in the story of The Lord of the Rings. The rest of The Silmarillion gives a lengthy account of the history of the world from its creation under Eru, the Father of All, the creation and history of elves, men, and dwarves, to the final battle in The Lord of the Rings and the passing of the elves, Gandalf, and Frodo to Valinor, the immortal land of the archangels, which God has hidden from the eyes of man.

Throughout this mythology, Tolkien does not explicitly mention the words *God* and *angel*, but, in effect, this is exactly what he is talking about in his books. He works, however, in a mythological, fantasy context that has many of the qualities of a legend and a fairy tale. Instead of God, he talks of The One or the Father of All in *The Silmarillion*. Instead of using the English word *angels*, he uses the elvish languages to call the archangels the *Ainur*, and the lesser angels, he calls the *Maiar*. In fact, in a letter to a friend, published in the preface to *The Silmarillion*, Tolkien says his creation story is meant to be a revelation of God and the "angelic powers, whose function is to exercise delegated authority in their spheres of rule and government, not [sic] creation, making or remaking."[2] Furthermore, in the creation story itself, God tells the archangels that he has animated them with "the Flame Imperishable,"[3] a term Tolkien uses to symbolically refer to the Holy Spirit. In fact, in both the book and the movie of *The Fellowship of the Ring*, Gandalf describes himself as the "servant of the Secret Fire"[4] when he dramatically faces the Balrog, a demon serving Morgoth and Sauron.

Tolkien's origin myth is not meant to replace the creation story in Genesis. Nor does it describe the origin of "the Word made flesh" from the book of John in the New Testament, much less the story of the gospel of Jesus Christ in the New Testament. Rather, it serves more like an elvish creation story that uses the elvish language to represent the creation of earth and the origin of the mythological lands in which the elves and the other races of Middle Earth live. Nothing in the story contradicts anything that the Bible explicitly says about God or his angels.

The rest of the saga in *The Silmarillion* and The Lord of the Rings describes the conflicts of elves, dwarves, and men with one another and with the satanic forces of Morgoth and Sauron. Although the story does not mention Jesus Christ, it does point to man's need for salvation and points ahead to Christ's vicarious atonement, much as Genesis 3:15 points forward to the Messiah, the "seed of the woman" who will crush Satan's rule after being wounded by Satan. Beyond this verse, and some allegorical meanings, Genesis does not contain explicit references to Jesus Christ or to the Trinity either, for that matter; yet Christians have not rejected that book out of hand, as some have done with Lord of the Rings.

There are other Christian symbols in The Lord of the Rings. For example, Frodo is a Christ-figure who takes on the burden of sin and temptation, symbolized by the evil ring, and casts it into a symbolic lake of fire, as represented by the fires of Mount Doom. Like Jesus Christ, Frodo shows grace and mercy to the fallen creature Gollum. Gollum, a kind of doppelganger for Frodo, becomes an unwilling instrument in the success of Frodo's mission but falls to his death in an abyss. Ultimately, therefore, it is grace and mercy that save Frodo from a similar fate.

Grace and mercy also save the world from the evil power of the ring and of Sauron. So in another sense Frodo can symbolize us as fallen beings, who are saved by the grace of God through Jesus Christ and who are admonished to become imitators of Christ so that the Holy Spirit may live through us. Like the believer, Frodo becomes a New Man who eventually travels to paradise, which the elves have named Valinor, or the Blessed Realm.

Sustaining Frodo and Sam on their way to Mount Doom is the lembas bread that the elves have given to them. This bread is a symbol of the body of Christ in the Eucharist that sustains a Christian's spiritual life and his relationship with Jesus Christ. During their perilous journey to Mount Doom, Frodo shows pity and mercy toward the creature Gollum, the former owner of the Ring of Power who has been corrupted by the evil ring. There is providence in Frodo's acts of mercy, for Gollum plays an important role in the final destruction of the ring. As Romans 8:28 tells us, "In all things God works for the good of those who love Him." In other words, what Gollum meant for evil, God in his providence used for good.

To create a Christ-figure in literature, you do not need to have a complete representation of Jesus Christ's life, death, and resurrection. Nor do you need an explicit representation of the gospel of Jesus Christ. For example, some Christ-figures are redeemer-heroes rather than savior-heroes because they reflect Christ taking on human burdens and sinfulness in suffering but not to the point of a sacrificial death. There are additional kinds of Christ-figures—for example, the martyr-hero whose suffering and death witnesses to values and convictions (*Braveheart*) and the clown-figure who highlights the fact that God's folly is wiser than human wisdom (*Bruce Almighty*).

Unlike Harry Potter, Tolkien's The Lord of the Rings does not have a pagan, occult worldview. The power that Gandalf and the elves have is a supernatural power that originates in the power of God or Eru, the Father of All. This power is used sparingly and only for good, not for evil (though the characters are not perfect). This is not often true with regard to Harry Potter's use of witchcraft power. Furthermore, the magical power of the ring that Frodo bears to Mount Doom is an evil, corrupting power that all the good characters shun, except when they are tempted by their own desire for domination. The ultimate intent is to destroy this evil magic, and both Gandalf and the elven Queen Galadriel reject possession of the ring when Frodo offers it to them. Furthermore, one of the main goals in The Lord of the Rings is to save and redeem the current generation, which has fallen from its former glory. All of these positive qualities seem to contrast sharply with Harry Potter's pagan, anti-Christian worldview.

Finally, the charge that Tolkien advocated human reincarnation centers on a comment Tolkien once made that the immortal elves, if they die accidentally or in war, may eventually return to earth in a resurrected body. That statement has nothing to do with human reincarnation or Hindu ideas or New Age concepts of reincarnation. The humans in Tolkien's mythology can only die once; they cannot be reincarnated.

In discussing the worldview of a particular work, we need to be sensitive to the apparent intent of the author by looking at the heroes and the villains. Not every work will take a position on Christianity and religion, of course, but you can ask whether real consequences to sin are exposed. You can also ask how relationships and love are portrayed.

Tolkien's mythology includes the existence of a personal God who provides for his creatures. The heroes in his works are righteous, courageous, and humble. They display mercy, respect, and love for one another. The best of them also encourage one another to shun the magical power of the evil ring. The villains are prideful, tyrannical, destructive, and greedy for power, but real consequences to their sins are set forth. Finally the relationships between the heroes are positive. In fact, although Christianity is not mentioned, the image of the Fellowship of the Ring, which is on a holy quest, parallels that of the church under Christ. So despite what some critics say, the positive Christian attributes of Tolkien's mythology seem extraordinarily clear.

The Lord of the Rings and *The Silmarillion* clearly have a biblical view of the nature of being and of the physical universe and a biblical theology. They also have a strong Christian view of humans and the nature of sin. There is only one God who is the creator of a physical universe, which he fills with created beings, including angels and human beings. God's mandate for men and women is for them to establish a benevolent dominion over the earth. People are tempted and corrupted by evil, however; so God sends his angels to help deliver them from evil and lead them to God's moral and spiritual truth and goodness. Finally, like parts of the Hebrew Scriptures that foreshadow the incarnation, sacrifice, and resurrection of Jesus Christ, many aspects of the stories in Lord of the Rings and *The Silmarillion* also symbolize these Christological patterns, laying the groundwork for an explicit presentation of the gospel of Jesus Christ.

Let us now turn to a description and analysis of the movie versions of Tolkien's first two books, *The Fellowship of the Ring* and *The Two Towers*.

## THE FELLOWSHIP OF THE RING

New Line Cinema and director Peter Jackson have taken on a daunting task—how to turn one of the longest, most beloved novels of all time, The Lord of the Rings, into three epic movies that will do Christian author J. R. R. Tolkien's vision justice. The first of the three movies based on Tolkien's trilogy, *The Fellowship of the Ring*, arrived in movie theaters in December 2001.

Bottom line? *The Fellowship of the Ring* is a wonderful epic movie that vividly captures most of Tolkien's vision, including his moral theology and significant portions of his Christian vision for this fantasy.

Take your older children if they are mature enough to handle mystical creatures, frightening monsters, and sword fighting. Although the film contains no curse words, sex, or nudity, there is plenty of hacking of hideous Orcs (goblin-like creatures) to pieces, along with some very scary moments. There is also a thematic problem in one scene in the movie, a scene that was not explicitly in the first book of the trilogy.

In the story Frodo, a friendly, likeable hobbit played by Elijah Wood, is thrust into an incredible adventure not of his choosing. Gandalf, played magnificently by Ian McKellen, is a powerful "wizard" who helps Frodo destroy the ancient evil ring that has the power to unleash a hellish nightmare on the land. Middle Earth is a fantasyland populated by a variety of creatures that, though not evil, do not necessarily get along very well. After Frodo and some hobbit friends escape from the mysterious minions of the Dark Lord, a fellowship of these beings is cobbled together to help Frodo. They must take the ring into the enemy's territory to the fires of Mordor at Mount Doom, where the ring was created, to destroy it. Elves, hobbits, dwarves, and men must pull together in the face of literally monstrous odds to complete this task.

*The Fellowship of the Ring* succeeds as a movie in almost every way. Director Peter Jackson's art direction is superb. The lands of Mordor (the evil villain's land) and the Shire, as portrayed in this movie, are wondrous. Cities carved into the sides of mountains, giant statues, and ruins of civilizations past fill the frame. Clouds and mist, rain and snow add texture and a "reality" that draws the viewer into the story. Though a couple of the characters are spottily drawn despite the movie's three-hour length, Jackson also manages to convey the spirit of the fantasy characters created by Tolkien.

There is a very necessary, lyrical opening that tries to bring non-Tolkienites up to speed on the events prior to this movie. However, condensing *The Hobbit* and parts of *The Silmarillion* into two minutes is a little hard. Nevertheless, the director made a good try, and a non-Tolkienite can catch up fairly soon.

Hardcore "Rings" fans are never going to be completely happy though, because film can never capture an individual's exact interpretation of characters in a book. In several cases, the movie eclipsed our memory of certain scenes . . . and that was a thrill. Moreover, the movie will visually "fill out" the books for their fans—adding a new dimension to their experience. The key to the success of *The Fellowship of the Ring* is that director Peter Jackson makes the audience like the characters and care what happens to them. The incredible visuals and soundtrack are just icing on the cake.

What can Christians expect to receive from this movie? Well, it is very easy to spot wonderful analogies to the Christian faith. Gandalf is powerful, yet kind. He dispenses wisdom and has a good sense of humor. He states, "We cannot change what has been. It is what we do with the days we have that matters." Furthermore, he tells Frodo, "Don't be so free to deal in death and judgment." In other words, don't try to play God, which is the opposite of the philosophy of Harry Potter.

One of the other important characters helping Frodo on his quest is Aragorn (Strider). Aragorn is a king who has left his throne in search of himself and to avoid the temptation that corrupted his ancestors. He is a bold, brave, kind, and valiant warrior, very much like a King David running from Saul. Aragorn's act of humbling himself by rejecting the crown that is rightly his has Christological implications.

The wonderful way the Fellowship bands together to help each other, though they are strangers, is an example of the body of Christ working together. When one is wounded, the others rally around to protect him. It is a very powerful illustration of Christians helping their wounded brothers and sisters and pulling together to conquer the common enemy.

The evil ring itself represents the lure of sin. Anyone within its sphere of influence is tempted by its mysterious pull. Anyone weak of heart feels a type of hypnotic lust for power. One of the most powerful scenes in the movie is when the forest elf Queen Galadriel is alone with Frodo and is offered the ring. Frodo is tired and weary of constant danger and would be happy to have someone of more substance take it off his hands. Galadriel (who radiates a soft glow) confesses she has always dreamed of possessing it.

As she comes within the ring's power, almost touching it, she transforms into a ghostly, ghastly, larger version of herself and proclaims loudly, "I could be the queen of Middle Earth, and all would love and fear me!" (paraphrase). Frodo falls to the ground in fear. As quickly as she changed, she changes back. Now exhausted, she says softly, "I passed the test." Then she speaks about being able to continue her current rule. Thus, this beautiful queen has resisted the ultimate temptation—to be a god!

There are two problems, however, in this first part of The Lord of the Rings. Both these problems make the movie inappropriate for some, if not many, older children. First, the movie adds a brutal battle at the end that is not in the book. In the book the battle is only implied, but the movie-makers seem to enjoy depicting the brutality that occurs during that battle. Second, in one scene during the middle of the movie, Gandalf and another wizard battle each other with their magical staffs. Although the scenes surrounding this battle do indeed take place in the book, this battle doesn't. It could be argued that Gandalf's use of the staff here is similar to the kind of power that Moses manifests in using the staff that God empowered in Egypt. However, the scene resembles more a fight between two warlocks or witches and may confuse people regarding the differences between a biblical and an occult worldview. This battle scene shows that the filmmakers do not always retain the Christian worldview that permeates Tolkien's masterpiece.

Finally, those who do not like sword fighting should stay away. Hard-core Tolkien fans should go easy and enjoy director Jackson's interpretation of a literary masterpiece. He said it best in a magazine interview: "We aren't burning the books. If you don't like the movie, just go back to the books." Furthermore, the movie will encourage this new generation to read the books, which is better than playing video games any day. *Fellowship of the Ring* comes through as wonderful, exciting entertainment. It is a movie worthy of Christian support.

## THE TWO TOWERS

The second Lord of the Rings movie is another wonderful Christmas present from Hollywood. Regrettably, however, it has a few more script and worldview problems. These problems slightly diminish Tolkien's metaphorical Christian vision.

*The Two Towers* opens magnificently with an eye-popping shot of Gandalf, played by Ian McKellen, struggling with the Balrog demon as they tumble into a miles-long abyss. Suddenly the movie cuts to Frodo and his gardener Sam traveling to Lord Sauron's evil kingdom. They manage to capture Gollum, the former hobbit who used to own the ring and is now trying to get it back. Despite Sam's protests, Frodo displays mercy toward this pitiful creature. Gollum then promises to help them find a secret, albeit dangerous, path into the land of Mordor.

As Frodo, Sam, and Gollum make their way into this terrible land, their former companions, the human named Aragorn, the dwarf Gimli, and the elf Legolas are chasing a small army of demon-like Orcs. The Orcs have kidnapped the other two hobbits, Merry and Pippin, and are taking them to the evil "wizard" Saruman. This "wizard" is pretending to be in league with Sauron, though he really wants the powerful evil ring all for himself.

Before they can free Merry and Pippin, the pursuers run into horsemen from the human kingdom of Rohan. The horsemen say they have already defeated the small army of Orcs. Aragorn, Gimli, and Legolas think the hobbits have died in the battle, but they go to make sure. They find that the hobbits escaped during the battle to run into the dark and mysterious forest of Fangorn. There the hobbits discover an unexpected ally and soon uncover an exciting bit of good news: Gandalf has mysteriously been resurrected and "sent back" to help them at the turning of the tide. Gandalf leads Aragorn, Legolas, and Gimli into a desperate battle to save the kingdom of Rohan and its king from Saruman's evil machinations and massive armies.

While all of this happens, Gollum leads Frodo and Sam through the marshes of the dead. A couple of surprises lie in store for them in the land of Mordor, not the least of which is Gollum's apparent reform, which teeters on the razor's edge.

It is a known fact of scriptwriting, seldom discussed, that the second act of a script is the most difficult. Although some aficionados think the second book in The Lord of the Rings trilogy is the best, it is not easily translated into the dramatic elements of the cinematic arts. To achieve a crisis, climax, and resolution, Peter Jackson and his team have done a yeoman's job of telescoping events, adding several elements and tweaking storylines.

However, even though this is a four-star movie, there are several points where all the elements do not add up, where the plot wanders, and where the characters get in their own way—which may distract a few viewers. On the other hand, Jackson's rendition of *The Two Towers* may leave others in a fog of cinematic bliss.

It is really hard to pick out one or two cast members because practically everyone gives a very good performance. That said, the highlight of the acting this time around may be Viggo Mortensen's strong performance as Aragorn, Liv Tyler as the elf lady Arwen, Sean Astin as Sam,

John Rhys-Davies as Gimli, and Andy Serkis as the voice of Gollum. Serkis also performed most of Gollum's movements for the computer special effects. The computer effects give an excellent, naturalistic texture to Gollum's body and set a new standard for computer animation.

Although *The Two Towers* generally keeps to the strong moral course Tolkien set, it does not do as good a job of highlighting some of the redemptive aspects. For example, there's a New Agey resurrection shot of Gandalf, whose hair and raiment have turned almost completely white from his experience of death and resurrection. The movie version also heightens the environmentalist notions that appear in Tolkien's masterpiece. Regrettably, this may encourage people to divorce resurrection and respect for nature from the Christian fantasy context in which Tolkien placed them. While in The Lord of the Rings, nature could turn malevolent, the movie versions of the book downplay this possibility; so Christians should be aware of this when viewing these movies.

Even so, the moral message of *The Two Towers* has peculiar relevance for us today. Like the characters in Tolkien, we are faced with an epic struggle against evil, not only against terrorism and terrorist states but also against the evil within ourselves and in the daily world in which we live. *The Two Towers* suggests that war is sometimes necessary and even desirable. Like the character Wormtongue who tries to convince the king of Rohan not to fight, this secular culture pressures Christians to avoid taking a stand, to be careful about angering others, to avoid mentioning anything about the culture war, and even to refrain from talking about Jesus Christ because it offends people.

Like the tree herders in *The Two Towers*, people in the real world must decide which side they are on. As Jesus Christ said more than once, we are either for God or against him; we are either for evil or against it. Some issues are, indeed, black and white, and sometimes there is no middle ground. Scripture admonishes us to fight evil with good however.

*The Two Towers* contains many strong fighting scenes. Also the creatures that Saruman and Sauron have bred are too scary for younger children and for many older children as well. Included among these elements are a very quick shot of an Orc's arm being cut off and cannibalism among the Orcs, who also talk of tasting "man flesh" and eating the hobbits. Tolkien's book, however, also mentions some of these things. Like the movies, Tolkien's Lord of the Rings is mostly meant for teenagers and adults who love action adventure stories, including massive, exciting (and violent) battle scenes. However, the audience will not find the kind of blood and gore that occurs in movies such as *Saving Private Ryan* and *We Were Soldiers*.

Finally, like Tolkien's book, Jackson's version consists of cinematic parallel editing, switching back and forth between different subplots. Although this is a time-honored technique, with which D. W. Griffith amazed audiences during the age of silent movies, it makes the story too choppy at times and a bit rushed, especially with all the running around that the characters do. In the long run, these are small flaws in an epic work that will not be fully realized until New Line Cinema releases part three, *The Return of the King*.

## THE HERO'S JOURNEY

Near the end of the movie version of *The Two Towers*, Frodo's faithful companion Sam gives a heartfelt speech about the stories they heard as youths. Sam's speech takes place at a moment when Frodo expresses total despair. The burden of carrying the evil ring has become too much for him. He tells Sam, "I can't go on." Sam lifts Frodo's spirit by reminding him of the stories of their youth, tales of great heroic deeds. The heroes in those stories often come to a point where everything seems lost, Sam says. Yet those heroes carried on because they believed, deep down, that there is still some good in the world.

This scene is an implicit expression of faith in the providence of God, who will not abandon his children, no matter how dark things seem to be. It also evokes the power of stories and myths to honor what's best in this world and to inspire people in all areas of their lives. A brief glance at the most successful films at the worldwide box office reveals that most of them—including *Spider-Man, Star Wars, Independence Day, The Fellowship of the Ring, The Two Towers*, and *Jurassic Park*—reflect this desire of people to be inspired by uplifting stories, myths, and fairy tales.

Many stories focus on a heroic figure who overcomes trials and tribulations to defeat some kind of evil or to attain some kind of valuable, positive goal. In stories and myths, the hero or heroine undergoes a rite of passage or initiation that leads to a change of status for him or her. During this rite of passage, the main character encounters various situations that test his or her character, courage, stamina, strength, and inner resolve. This test of character can affect his or her spiritual, intellectual, psychological, social, and ethical development.

This is exactly what happens to both Frodo and Sam. They are heroes, but because of their humble origins, they also appeal to the average person. Their moral fiber, compassion, and faith in providence help them overcome insurmountable obstacles and extraordinary situations. By the end of Tolkien's third book, *The Return of the King*, their spiritual, intellectual, psychological, social, and ethical abilities have grown greatly. Tolkien has used these fictional characters to portray his Christian worldview in a heroic, literary fashion full of transcendental, spiritual significance. Because of this, his stories have become a tremendous inspiration to millions of people. This fact, and so much more, is what has made the Lord of the Rings books and movies among the most successful, most popular works of all time.

For the same reasons the stories of the Bible inspire millions of people, including those who ultimately may reject God or may not come to Christ. Of course, fictional stories about heroes cannot replace the inspiring stories in the Bible, which show God actively working in real history to redeem and empower his fallen children. In the Bible we not only encounter inspiring biblical heroes, but we can also personally encounter the living God, who "causes all things to work together for good to those who love God" (Rom. 8:28 NASB). In that way, the Bible ultimately becomes the model for our own heroic journey through life. Even though we walk through the valley of the shadow of death, we will fear no evil, for God is with us; his rod and staff will comfort us. And we will dwell in the house of the Lord forever (Ps. 23). In the end, the Bible is the best legacy families can leave their children, grandchildren, and the future generations to come. It has the ultimate ring of truth.

Below are some media-wise questions for children, teenagers, and adults who read or see The Lord of the Rings. Please note that wisdom involves, in part, understanding the consequences of your actions. These questions are intended to promote wisdom. Please add any questions that you find relevant for your child.

1. Why is a humble hobbit rather than a powerful wizard chosen for this mission?

2. Why is it important that Gandalf says that we cannot change what has been, but "it is what we do with the days we have that matters"?

3. Why is it important that Frodo is told not to be so quick to "deal in death and judgment"?

4. Why was it important to reject the temptation of the ring's power?

5. Why does Galadriel, the elf queen, reject the ring and say that she "passed the test"?

6. In what ways is selfishness rebuked in the movie?

7. How does the movie show the difference between right and wrong?

8. What happens when Pippin and Merry disobey?

9. How does the ring corrupt people?

10. What is the biblical worldview of The Lord of the Rings?

11. Why is a biblical worldview important?

12. What is the good news in the story?

# IV

# COSMIC BATTLES FOR BEAUTY, VIRTUE, AND HONOR

*For though we walk in the flesh, we are not waging war according to the flesh. For the weapons of our warfare are not of the flesh but have divine power to destroy strongholds. We destroy arguments and every lofty opinion raised against the knowledge of God, and take every thought captive to obey Christ.*

2 CORINTHIANS 10:3

Jesus Christ knew the power of stories to teach, influence, and inspire when he spoke to his disciples in parables—the Good Samaritan, the prodigal son, and the rich man and Lazarus. Parables are short fictitious stories illustrating a moral principle or a religious doctrine.

Books and movies are like parables in that they too can illustrate moral principles and religious doctrines, including beliefs about God and Jesus Christ. Even an atheist writer, filmmaker, or television producer has a belief about God—he or she doesn't believe God exists.

Of course, Jesus Christ told parables that in the Christian worldview taught moral principles and religious doctrines that are good, true, and beautiful. Therefore, Christians believe that all stories should teach the good, the true, and the beautiful. They also believe that stories should not contradict what the Bible teaches, including the moral principles given to Moses by God and those given by Jesus and his disciples in the New Testament documents. Christians furthermore believe that stories should not contradict what the New Testament teaches about Jesus Christ. They also recognize that, except for the human writers of the New Testament documents, who were perfectly inspired by God and enlightened by his Holy Spirit, all stories are made by fallible human beings and thus reflect the sinful, error-prone nature of humanity. In taking this approach, it is good to note what Paul says in 1 Timothy 4:7 (NIV): "Have nothing to do with godless myths and old wives' tales; rather, train yourself to be godly." Notice that this passage does not say to reject all stories or all traditional folktales—only those that are godless and false.

Many Christian denominations and churches have strayed from this biblical, Christ-centered worldview. They don't accept some or many of the teachings of the Bible and the New Testament. Their beliefs may or may not contradict an essential teaching necessary for their salvation, but often they try to rationalize their beliefs by saying that the biblical understanding of a particular issue is historically or scientifically flawed. Although they may hold on to some, and even many or most, essential teachings of the Bible, their understanding of important issues seems cloudy at best, or heretical at worst.

Something similar is happening with regard to the Harry Potter books and movies. Some Christians who like the books or are not concerned about their possible effects on children maintain that the witchcraft in Harry Potter either is not the same kind of occult magic practiced by modern-day witches and neo-pagans or is not the same kind condemned by the Bible. Other Christians disapprove of Harry Potter, but they also condemn The Lord of the Rings because it contains a fantasy mythology independent of the Bible's creation story and its depiction of human history. These Christians cite the fact that both the good Gandalf and the evil Saruman are called "wizards," and the supernatural powers expressed in the books and movies are called "magical." Finally, still other Christians unnecessarily try to terrify parents by insisting that children who read Harry Potter or watch the movies are in tremendous danger of becoming ensnared by satanic witchcraft rituals or pagan cults.

All three of these positions are flawed.

First, although Harry Potter is a series of fantasy stories for children that exaggerates the idea of witchcraft in a whimsical, frequently humorous, but adventurous way, we, the authors, fail to see a substantial, material difference between the witchcraft and sorcery in Harry Potter and the practices condemned by the Bible. Deuteronomy 18:10-12 condemns both sorcery and divination, both witchcraft and the casting of spells, and it condemns people, mediums, and spiritists who consult dead people.

Contrary to what Harry Potter's defenders say, all of these evil things are part and parcel of the occult sorcery that occurs in Harry Potter. Furthermore, all of these practices actually do indeed occur within many versions of modern-day forms of witchcraft, neo-paganism, and/or spiritism. If you go to the Scholastic Books website on the Internet, one of the Harry Potter pages will refer you to the Scholastic Books website for its T*WITCH books and products, based on a series involving two twins who practice witchcraft and neo-paganism. One of the T*WITCH pages encourages children to send in their own spells, including protection spells, love spells, and homework spells. When we looked at that page on June 10, 2003, we found an eleven-year-old girl, Kiki, from Illinois who wrote, "Sun and Moon, Sea and Fire, let me have my desire." We also found a twelve-year-old from Texas, named Liz, who wrote another spell that said, in part, "O goddess of night" and "Mighty sun god."[1] Another Scholastic Books page on the Internet encourages schoolchildren in grades three and above: "Write your own magic spell."[2] Also Warner Brothers' Harry Potter website offers a CD-ROM for *Harry Potter and the Sorcerer's Stone* that enables children to "attend classes" at Hogwarts School of Witchcraft and Wizardry and learn spells.

According to novelist Michael D. O'Brien:

A recent search of the internet for Harry Potter references yielded more than 500,000 "hits" or sites where the books are being discussed, including those of major libraries. Selective searches turned up more than a hundred high-profile websites devoted to the series, many of which offer cross-links to advanced occult websites under titles such as "Learn More about the Secrets of the Occult" and "How to Become a Witch." In an interview with *Newsweek*, a spokesman for the Pagan Federation in England reported that he receives an average of 100 inquiries a month from young people who want to become witches—an unprecedented phenomenon which he attributes in part to the Potter books. An article in the December 17, 2000, issue of *Time* magazine reports that a similar organization in Germany deals with an increasing number of inquiries, which it also credits to the Potter factor. Rowling herself has expressed surprise at the volume of mail she receives from young readers writing to her as if Hogwarts were real, wanting to know how they can enter the school in order to become witches and wizards.

Librarians in diverse social settings report that children in increasing numbers are requesting material from the occult sections of their collections.[3]

Given these facts, why is it beyond the pale to believe that some children and teenagers who get involved in the fantasy world of Harry Potter might not be swept up into the practices and beliefs of modern-day witchcraft and paganism? What guarantees can Warner Brothers, Scholastic Books, your local school board, or J. K. Rowling give us that many children and teenagers will not be tempted to do such a thing?

Now we can imagine someone saying, "Kids play cops and robbers, but that doesn't make them turn to a life of crime." This would be an ignorant comment. In the game of cops and robbers, the robbers are the bad guys, but in the game of Harry Potter, the witches and sorcerers are the good guys. The people who can't, who don't, or who refuse to use occult magic are seen as the bad guys. In effect, Harry Potter turns good into evil and evil into good! This is thoroughly abhorrent.

O'Brien underlines the problem with these attitudes:

It is now almost universally taken for granted that we can absorb a certain amount of immoral entertainment without being adversely affected by it. We simply assume that if we have sufficient rational faith, we will be able to sift through good and bad material without being harmed by it, ignoring the bad, savoring the good. We numbly watch the graphically dramatized murders of many human beings every week. . . . We are entertained by television programs based on the occult worldview . . . and comedy programs . . . deriving enjoyment from the wit but little realizing how a diet of laughing at what is profoundly unfunny will over time alter our ability to understand the gravity of immoral acts. In short, we have accepted the normalcy of corruption. . . .

Books and films which three generations ago would have been instantly recognized as unhealthy for our children, are now considered acceptable, and those who oppose them alarmist or "hysterical." . . .

The hard question we must ask ourselves at this point in history, is to what degree have our judgments been influenced by "imperceivable influences on the subconscious." The record of our hits and misses in the area of discernment offers something of an answer: For example, reasonable Christian parents would not permit their children to read a series of enthralling books depicting the rites and adventures of likable young people involved in drug-dealing, or premarital sex, or sadism. We are still capable of recognizing the falsehood in glamorizing torture, because physical pain is a reality in everyone's life and anyone unjustly inflicting pain is instantly recognized for what he is—an enemy. We would not give our children fiction in which a group of "good fornicators" struggled against a set of "bad fornicators," because we know that the power of disordered sexual impulse is an abiding problem in human affairs, the negative effects of which we can see all around us. Why, then, have we accepted a set of books which glamorize and normalize occult activity, even though it is every bit as deadly to the soul as sexual sin, if not more so? Is it because we have not yet awakened to the fact that occultism is in fact a clear and present danger?

Why . . . do we presume that a sensually powerful series of children's books will not affect a young reader's interests and activities? Why have we come to assume that such novels have no consequences, that the experience of plunging the imagination into that alternative, and ultimately false world, will remain sealed in an airtight compartment of the mind? We must ask ourselves how we arrived at a position where we allow our children to absorb for hours on end, in the form of powerful fiction, activities that we would never permit them to observe or to practice in real life.[4]

On the other hand, those who condemn even Tolkien's work because of its magic do not understand the nature and purpose of this work of fiction. Tolkien's mythology and his Lord of the Rings novel take place in a fantasy realm in a mythical past where the honorable and humble hobbits, elves, dwarves, and men are helped by supernatural powers derived from God to defeat supernatural powers that have turned evil and demonic in rebellion against God. Furthermore, in Tolkien's world, which is a real physical world that cannot be manipulated by sheer mental or occult power, sin has real consequences. Finally, Tolkien's fantasy is not meant to take the place of biblical history, but is intended to point toward the Bible, toward God, and toward Christianity in an allegorical fashion. Thus, in *The Silmarillion* and The Lord of the Rings, there is Christian symbolism referring to the creation and providence of God the Father, as well as symbolic metaphors for the Holy Spirit and for Jesus Christ.

Tolkien created his fantasy stories in the spirit of the heroic myths, legends, and romances of the past, but imbued them with a strong Christian spin. Because of this, he infuses his heroes with a grace and civility that are truly inspirational.

Third, while Satan is behind all forms of non-Christian belief systems, so is willful human sin and rebellion against God. Thus some forms of witchcraft and neo-paganism are more dangerous than others. Many self-proclaimed witches and neo-pagans laugh at the idea that they advocate Satanism and demonism. They protest that very few, if any, of them consciously worship Satan. In fact, even most Satanists do not actually and consciously worship the devil or Satan, but are just licentious hedonists who use these personas to mock and snub their noses at Bible-believing Christians. Some modern-day witches and neo-pagans also point out that they may refer to such things as the "Mother Goddess" and her consort, the "Horned God," or talk about other gods and goddesses, including the Moon God or the Sun God, but they do not really believe in the existence of these deities and spirits. They are merely using these deities and spirits as symbolic references and fantasies in order to honor, love, and commune with nature.

In reality modern-day witchcraft and paganism is a diverse, amorphous collection of pagan cults, heathen religions, New Age cults, practitioners of witchcraft, Wiccan pagans, Wiccan witches or sorcerers, feminist cults, self-proclaimed Satanists, and solitary practitioners. The techniques practiced and taught by this diverse collection include a host of things, including divination, clairvoyance, spell-casting, spirit channeling, herbal healing, astral projection, and spiritism. Their actual beliefs can also be diverse and include such things as animism (attributing conscious life to objects in nature, phenomena in nature, or inanimate objects), polytheism (the worship of many gods), henotheism (the worship of one god among many), pantheism (the belief that everything is god), some form of deism (the belief that a god has become removed from his subjects), etc., or a combination thereof.

Many witches and neo-pagans do seem to accept the notion of human reincarnation and karma, the belief that the things we do in this life will affect us in a reincarnated life. This Americanized belief in reincarnation and karma seems to have its sources in the occultism and spiritism that gained popularity in the late 1800s and early 1900s, in particular with the Theosophy movement and the teachings of such people as Edgar Cayce. Radical feminism, especially the kind that falsely and often viciously attacks the alleged patriarchal doctrines in the Bible and Christianity, also has influenced the neo-pagan movement, as has the modern ecological movement. So a blending of different and even totally separate philosophical and religious beliefs and practices appears to be a chief characteristic of the neo-pagan movement. Sometimes it seems, in fact, that the only belief system excluded from this contradictory pagan and occult morass is Christianity, especially any form of Christianity that takes the Bible seriously.

Even so, Christians must be careful in making rash comparisons between Harry Potter, modern-day witchcraft, neo-pagan cults, and a demonized, inordinately powerful Satanism. We must avoid a conspiratorial view of this matter, even though we know that modern-day witchcraft, neo-pagan cults, and Satanists have one thing in common—they hate God, and they hate the children of God.

With this cautionary note, Christian and Jewish parents should continue to object vociferously to Harry Potter, modern-day witchcraft, and neo-paganism being shoved down children's throats by giant corporations and a government bureaucracy of well-meaning but misguided teachers and librarians. These government and business people have no problem with schoolchildren fantasizing about becoming Harry Potter at Hogwarts or using witchcraft. Ironically, many of these same teachers and librarians, and many neo-pagans, scream to high heaven when a Christian wants to put any of the Ten Commandments on a school bulletin board or when a Christian student wants to mention God or Jesus Christ in an academic paper or at a graduation ceremony.

Christians should be willing to objectively point out the very real dangers of Harry Potter while at the same time avoiding hysteria and emotional arguments. We do not have to raise the terrifying specter of satanic rituals, bloody human sacrifices, and demons. We do not have to distort the beliefs of modern-day witches and pagan cults to take a firm stand against the witchcraft and occult paganism taught in Harry Potter. In fact, that's the kind of thing that many of the witches and neo-pagans do in their hysterical ranting against Christianity, the church, and Bible-believing Christians.

For example, years ago I (Tom) went with some friends to witness to New Agers at an environmentalist fair in San Francisco. We passed out some tracts and articles about Christianity and the nature of truth at a booth we had rented. One day a scruffy-looking individual in a T-shirt stormed the booth, screaming about the evils of the Roman Catholic Church in the Middle Ages.

"But we're not Catholic; we're Protestants," we kept trying to tell the young man as we tried to engage him in a calm discussion.

The man wouldn't listen, however. He kept ranting and raving incoherently about Roman Catholicism until he got tired and walked away.

Of course, we would not behave so irrationally when debating somebody with a different worldview. Some Christians have, however, passed on unverified rumors about non-Christians—for example, the false rumor about an atheist group allegedly petitioning the federal government to censor the mention of God or Jesus Christ on public television airwaves. On the other hand, a recently proposed regulation in Great Britain actually would have outlawed Christian ownership of television stations, and some governments are writing "hate speech" laws censoring certain religious viewpoints, such as the Bible's firm, total command against homosexual behavior. The price of liberty is eternal vigilance, but so is the price of our freedom of speech. If we abuse our freedom of speech by spreading untruths, false rumors, and slander against groups and beliefs we oppose, we may encourage our enemies to deprive us of free speech altogether.

## A DIFFERENCE THAT MAKES A DIFFERENCE

As we have shown above, only minor differences exist between the exaggerated witchcraft of Harry Potter and the witchcraft condemned by God. Also there is little difference between Harry's witchcraft and most of the kinds of witchcraft in the neo-pagan movement.

The Harry Potter movies have a pagan worldview with very strong occult content. They may inspire children to dabble in witchcraft, sorcery, divination, and talking with dead people and other "spirits." The Word of God condemns (in Deuteronomy 18:10-12 and elsewhere) these beliefs and practices because they are ultimately demonic and satanic in origin. In addition to worshiping the earth and opposing Christianity and the Bible, some or even many witches and neo-pagans advocate sexual immorality, including homosexuality, and also believe in abortion as a sacred act. Without proper parental supervision, your child may succumb to these anti-Christian, anti-biblical beliefs and drift toward a hedonistic or pagan lifestyle that denies the power of God and the truth of the Bible. Harry Potter and the advertising and media hype surrounding the series also may inspire your child or teenager into investigating the many witchcraft websites on the Internet that attempt to repackage the very real dangers of witchcraft and paganism in order to inculcate young minds with tales of other "gods" and "goddesses," sorcery, sexual hedonism, and worse.

Although he has many good qualities, Harry Potter's disobedience, lying, and propensity to break the rules and seek revenge set him against the biblical model of a righteous hero. Furthermore, Harry has supernatural powers, which, contrary to the strained analogies made by some commentators, is not the case for any human child aside from Jesus Christ. Nor is it the case of any of the human characters in Lord of the Rings, nor of Frodo and Sam. That said, every human child is created by God with unique, sometimes brilliant talents and "gifts," and every child who comes to know Jesus Christ as Lord and Savior is filled with his Holy Spirit and the gifts that the Holy Spirit bestows on him or her. These gifts are not the same as the supernatural, paranormal powers of Harry and his friends.

There is a great deal of difference, however, between Harry Potter and the movies that Peter Jackson and his team of filmmakers have crafted from Christian author J. R. R. Tolkien's Lord of the Rings. The Lord of the Rings movies are a wonderful "epic" fantasy about good and evil with topnotch actors, storyline, and special effects. The movies are clean, and the filmmakers have left in plenty of Tolkien's biblical, allegorical Christian references, not to mention his strong, positive, moral worldview. They have fashioned a masterful blend of fantasy and adventure that has positive Christological implications.

In the first two Lord of the Rings movies, the family is portrayed in a positive way. For example, Faramir expresses concern for his brother Boromir; Arwen has great respect for her caring father Elrond; King Theoden deeply regrets that he let Saruman and Wormtongue, Saruman's human compatriot, poison his mind, resulting in the death of his son.

Harry Potter's family members, by contrast, are so mean that he must escape them and find a home away from them at Hogwarts School. Harry and his friends too often escape adult supervision, which sets a bad example for children to follow. Contrast this behavior with the children in Helm's Deep in *The Two Towers* where the parents of the children protect them and help them.

"Good triumphs over evil" is clearly the premise in The Lord of the Rings trilogy, where the good is represented by grace, mercy, honor, loyalty, and love, and the evil is represented by the magical ring that tempts all creatures to sin or rebel against God. The premise in Harry Potter is that the more powerful, more attractive wizard defeats the less powerful, less attractive one. As such, Harry Potter's premise reflects a gnostic worldview that is dualistic—a clear contradiction of Scripture.

The gnostic, occult worldview of Harry Potter portrays evil as having tremendous power and says that the hero can only succeed by participating in occult power. The Lord of the Rings portrays evil as something that no one would want to imitate and shows that rebellion, disobedience, and sin have negative consequences.

The Lord of the Rings makes biblically sound moral statements— that humility, loyalty, mercy, and commitment are to be valued, there are some good things worth fighting for, and there is a divine plan. In Harry Potter disobeying rules is praiseworthy if successful, family and school rules are restrictive, deception may be a necessary means to an end, and playing tricks on others is justified if funny.

Christians and Jews believe in a real epistemology, which means that they know because God tells them. He has told us that his laws govern all creation, including the forest; so we know that the life and death of trees occurs because trees are subject to his laws. The Lord of the Rings has this real epistemology.

Many media products, including Harry Potter, set forth the view that you cannot know and therefore are trapped in an unpredictable and frightening world. The ultimate reality for these nominalists (which means that the things in the world are only names—not real things) is merely a fiction and not the real creation of a real God. This nominalistic ontology, or view of the nature of being, denies the reality of sin and the need for salvation. A nominalist premise also blurs the line between imagination and reality.

In the Christian, biblical worldview, however, evil is real, and denying its reality by saying that it is only a dream or an illusion denies the need for Jesus' death on the cross to save us from our sins and from sin itself. While Christians and Jews believe we live in a real world, they do not subscribe to the materialistic view of humanists and communists—that all that exists is the material world and that the spiritual world is merely an invention of deluded minds.

The biblical view is that we live in a real world, created by the real God, where there are real problems, real pain, and real suffering that we cannot ignore or wish away. For those of us who are Christians, the creator God has saved us from real evil, sin, and death through the real death and resurrection of his Son, Jesus the Christ, who was really God and really man. Any other ontology denies this gospel.

Every movie has an ontology whether the producer, writer, or director knows it or not. The first two Harry Potter books and movies present a nominalistic, occult, gnostic ontology filled with magical thinking that is contrary to the Word of God, though these products have a moral conclusion. The Lord of the Rings has a real ontology where there are real consequences for Frodo and the other characters' actions, real death, and real solutions that require taking moral responsibility.

Although The Lord of the Rings certainly is not a perfect work, there is a real difference between it and the Harry Potter stories. It's a real difference that makes a difference.

## THE COSMIC BATTLE

The Bible clearly teaches us that we are in a cosmic battle for the souls of our children and our nations. It is a battle for the true, the good, and the beautiful. It is also a battle for justice, virtue, and honor.

The players in this cosmic battle are God—the ultimate source of all truth, justice, goodness, and beauty, who sent his Son Jesus Christ to sacrifice himself for our sins and crush the head of Satan—and humanity, which is torn between its sinful nature and the call of God to turn away from sin and return to him. Each of us, in his or her individual way, shares the ordeal of Jesus Christ when he was tempted by Satan in the wilderness.

If you remember, in the description of that historical conflict in Matthew 4, Jesus was "full of the Holy Spirit." The Spirit led Jesus into the desert where he ate nothing for forty days and became very hungry.

The devil came to Jesus in the desert and told him to turn a stone into bread to assuage his hunger. Jesus refused and quoted Deuteronomy 8:3 of the Hebrew Scriptures: "Man does not live on bread alone, but on every word that comes from the mouth of God."

Then the devil took Jesus to the highest point of the temple in Jerusalem and told Jesus to throw himself over the edge and command his angels to save him. Jesus refused and quoted Deuteronomy 6:16: "Do not put the Lord your God to the test."

Finally, the devil showed Jesus all the splendor of the kingdoms of the world. "All this I will give you," the devil said, "if you will bow down and worship me." Jesus replied, quoting Deuteronomy 6:13, "Away from me, Satan! For it is written: 'Worship the Lord your God, and serve him only.'"

Faced with this strong biblical opposition, the devil left Jesus, and angels came and attended him (Matthew 4:11 NIV).

This narrative passage may be one of the most important in all of holy Scripture. Whenever the devil tempted Jesus to sin, Jesus, who was filled with the Holy Spirit, put the focus back on God and on God's Word. Furthermore, when the devil finally left empty-handed, God's angels came and ministered to Jesus. There is real power in God and in God's Word, and Jesus relied on that power.

In the same way, as we ourselves go about our daily struggles, from the greatest to the smallest, we too can be ministered to by God's angels if we are filled with the Holy Spirit and if we focus on God and on his Word. That is the best way to have victory over the devil, wicked people, and our own sinful nature, which is emblematic of the devil's power.

Here we have then a sacred story, full of the power of God, that can teach, influence, and inspire us throughout our whole lives. It is a perfect example of the power of the storytelling gift that God has placed in our hands. God can use this powerful tool to lead us toward the purity, righteousness, nobility, and love that Paul mentions in Philippians 4:8 in the New Testament. However, stories can also be a powerful tool for satanic powers, including sinful human beings who have rebelled against God and who have rejected the Word of God and the gospel of Jesus Christ.

Harry Potter and The Lord of the Rings are part of this epic struggle, this cosmic battle for the true, the good, and the beautiful. Despite some positive aspects, the Harry Potter series is a work whose pagan, occult, gnostic, and nominalistic worldview points us toward sin and rebellion and ultimately denies the gospel of Jesus Christ. Despite some imperfections, The Lord of the Rings books and movies point us toward God and Jesus Christ and toward truth, honor, virtue, and beauty.

Ultimately, it is God as he has revealed himself through the Bible who is the final standard by which we should live. God is the Rock that lifts us high and protects us from the foes without and within. As Psalm 62:1-2, 11-12 (NIV) tells us, "My soul finds rest in God alone; my salvation comes from him. He alone is my rock and my salvation; he is my fortress, I will never be shaken. . . . you, O God, are strong, and . . . you, O Lord, are loving. Surely you will reward each person according to what he has done." Therefore, we should put our trust in God at all times and pour out our hearts to him (Psalm 62:8).

This, then, is the spiritual approach we should take while we protect our homes and communities from the negative influences of the entertainment media and while we continue working diligently to encourage the entertainment industry to adopt higher standards based on the Word of God.

# ◆PART◆
# TWO

# V

# PILLARS OF MEDIA WISDOM

*Anyone who thinks the media has nothing to do with this [the Columbine High School massacre] is an idiot.*

LESLIE MOONVES, PRESIDENT, CBS

Four out of every five parents think popular culture, such as music, television, and movies, negatively affects children.[1] Single parents especially say they need help shielding their children from the mass media of entertainment's emphasis on perverse sex, gruesome violence, and shrill obscenity.

Parents are concerned about popular culture because their children are being conformed in dress, actions, and ideas to the images of Hollywood idols like Britney Spears, Leonardo DiCaprio, Snoop Dogg, and Eminem, rather than to positive, moral images of virtuous men and women and, in particular, to the image of Jesus Christ.

Parents should be concerned. The mass media of entertainment are among the most influential teachers of our children. In the United States the average child sees 15,000 to 30,000 hours of television[2] by the time he or she is seventeen years old. During this same period a child spends only 11,000 to 16,000 hours in school,[3] and 2,000 hours or less of quality interaction with his or her parents.[4] Many American children spend more time with a television set before the age of six than they will spend with their fathers during their lifetime. Thus, television has the educational edge in terms of "class" time.

Furthermore, according to the Federal Trade Commission in a report released in 2000, 63 percent of American children age nine to seventeen said they find it "important" to see the latest movies. Also, children age eight to thirteen spend three hours per week on average at the movie theater. Finally, 62 percent of children age nine to seventeen report that they watch a video once a week or more.[5] No wonder the entertainment industry has such a huge impact on our families' lives!

## A PRIMARY TEACHER OF OUR YOUTH

Children learn in part when teachers present information and/or behavior, repeat the information and/or behavior, and reward the accurate feedback of the information and/or behavior. Television, videos, and movies present, repeat, and reward behavior and/or information much more often than parents and teachers do, not only because they occupy more of a child's time, but also because they are designed to deliver more information per second. Moreover, they often present, repeat, and reward more effectively than do parents or teachers because they are entertaining, exciting, and captivating.

To a greater or lesser degree, depending on the medium, electronic games, MTV, and the other entertainment media have the same type of educational impact as television. For example, electronic games allow the player to interact with the game, which provides a means of cognitive or mental growth and comprehensive education in the skills of the game.

It is important to understand that even though television, movies, and videos provide behavioral modeling and information, they fail to provide cognitive growth because cognitive growth requires interaction and reflection. Since cognitive growth is necessary in order to develop higher thinking skills, many educators do not consider television an educational tool. In fact, studies have shown that television, videos, and movies often hinder cognitive growth and may produce symptoms of learning deficiency in children. Therefore, many experts claim correctly that these media do not educate. At the same time, they do educate from a layperson's perspective in terms of behavior, psychological development, emotional development, and perception— often to the detriment of the viewer. Even those educators who focus on cognitive growth (the process of knowing and judging, which involves perception, awareness, thinking, discernment, and wisdom) agree that television can assist in educating if used properly in the classroom with other educational tools and techniques that aid mental development.

To comprehend this important distinction so that you are not confused by reports on this issue, two examples may suffice. Many parents have noticed that their baby may learn to say the word *daddy* and then call every person the child sees "daddy." It is only through interaction and reflection that the baby correctly identifies his father with the word *daddy*. Researchers and parents have also observed that young children will tend to hit each other while watching a violent television program. If the researcher or parent asks the child what he is watching, the child will respond, "I don't know." Because he is not reflecting on what he is watching, he is not growing cognitively.

## GO INTO ALL THE WORLD

Moms and dads worry about the influence of media violence on their children, but many don't know what to do about the problem. The good news is that there are effective ways to teach your children and teenagers to be media-wise.

As director of the TV Center at City University of New York, I (Ted) helped develop some of the first media literacy courses in the late 1970s. Since then years of research have produced a clear understanding of how to teach media literacy.

There are four pillars of media wisdom:

1. Understand the influence of the entertainment media;
2. Understand your child's cognitive development;
3. Understand how the entertainment media functions and its nature and grammar; and,

4. Understand your moral, spiritual values and teach them to your children.

Learning these four pillars can help you and your family navigate through the dangerous minefields and fragrant flowers of the pop culture landscape.

## THE INFLUENCE OF THE ENTERTAINMENT MEDIA

For many of us, recognizing media influence means coming out of denial. As Dale Kunkel, professor at the University of California, Santa Barbara, points out, after thousands of intensive studies in this area, only one significant researcher still denies the influence of the media, and that researcher last did real research in this area in the mid-1980s. In the wake of the Columbine High School massacre, CBS president Leslie Moonves put it quite bluntly: "Anyone who thinks the media has nothing to do with this is an idiot" (Associated Press, 5/19/99).[6] Thus, the American Psychological Association's report on media violence concludes, "There is absolutely no doubt that those who are heavy viewers of violence demonstrate increased acceptance of aggressive attitudes and increased aggressive behavior."[7]

Thousands of scientific studies and case studies have shown the powerful influence the entertainment media has on people's cognitive development and behavior, especially that of children, teenagers, and young people, who represent the largest audience. In fact, by the time they are seventeen years old, children will have spent at least 40,000 hours watching movies, videos, and TV programs, playing video games, listening to music, and reading popular books and news stories. But remember that these children spend only 11,000 hours in school and 2,000 hours with their parents. They spend 800 hours in church if they regularly attend! That's about 2,353 hours of media consumption per year for the average child. Our current figures indicate that up to 20 percent of this time, or about 471 hours, will feature a solid, strong, or very strong moral worldview. Up to 7 percent, or about 165 hours, will feature a solid, strong, or very strong redemptive or Christian worldview. Just who is teaching our youth can be seen by the following chart:

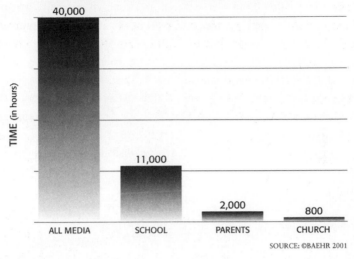

Who Teaches Our Children by the Time They Are 17?

SOURCE: ©BAEHR 2001

As you can see, the entertainment industry may have a bigger impact on children and society than parents and churches have.

Early in 2001 the surgeon general of the United States agreed with four top medical groups—American Medical Association, American Academy of Pediatrics, American Psychological Association, and the American Academy of Child and Adolescent Psychiatry, as well as countless psychological and neurological experts—that violence in the mass media is contributing to increased violent behavior among children and teenagers.[8] Not only that, but many scientific studies from other sources, such as education professor Diane Levin, author of *Remote Control Childhood? Combating the Hazards of Media Culture*,[9] and psychologists like Dr. Victor Cline, Dr. Stanley Rachman, Dr. Judith Reisman, and Dr. W. Marshall,[10] have found that viewing sexual images in the media has led to increased sexual activity among children and teenagers and increased deviant behavior, including rape. Furthermore, a recent Dartmouth Medical School study of New England middle-school students, reported by the National Cancer Institute, found that viewing drug use in movies and TV programs leads to increased drug use among children.[11]

A long-term study released in 2002 proved once again the negative effects of today's popular visual media on young people. Published in the journal *Science*, the study found that teenagers and young adults who watch more than one hour of television, including videos daily, are more likely to commit violent crimes and exhibit other forms of aggressive behavior. The study, led by Jeffrey G. Johnson of Columbia University and the New York State Psychiatric Institute, followed children in 707 families in two counties in northern New York state for seventeen years. Adolescents and young adults who watched television for more than seven hours per week had an increased likelihood of between 16 and 200 percent of committing an aggressive act in later years. The study found a link between violence and viewing any television, not just violent programming. "The evidence has gotten to the point where it's overwhelming," Johnson said.[12]

A ground-breaking Tufts University study released in January 2003 showed that television influences the behavior of children as young as twelve months old. In the study, ten-month-old and twelve-month-old infants watched a videotape of an actress reacting to a toy with a positive or negative emotion. When the actress appeared to be afraid of the toy, the babies avoided playing with it and appeared worried or even cried. When the actress enthusiastically played with the toy, the infants were more apt to play with it. Tufts child behavioral expert Dr. Donna Mumme noted, "It was quite striking to us that one-year-olds were able to gather that much information from a twenty-second television clip." Therefore, Dr. Mumme concluded, parents may want to "think twice before they let an infant see television programs meant for an older person."[13]

In other words, movies like *Hannibal, From Hell, Scream, American Wedding, Freddy Vs. Jason, The Matrix Reloaded, Queen of the Damned, Austin Powers in Goldmember,* and television programs like *Jackass, The Sopranos, The West Wing, Temptation Island,* and *Will & Grace* can have a tremendously negative impact on the lives of many children and teenagers, as well as their parents, families, friends, and teachers. These types of movies and programs are nothing more than *visual terrorism.*

Not only does the Hollywood-based mass media of entertainment influence our children, but it also influences people throughout the world. After the tragedy of the attack on the World Trade Center on September 11, 2001, Boston University undertook a study to determine the attitudes of people throughout the world toward Americans. Released in January 2003, this shocking study showed that young people around the world had a very negative image of Americans and that this image was in part responsible for the outpouring of hate on 9/11.[14] The study concluded that the dislike of the United States would grow over the next few years and that it is a response to the image of Americans being presented by Hollywood, not the real attributes of real Americans. In other words, Hollywood is our ambassador to the world.

The study found that good deeds done in the past do not count for much. Although it can be shown that the United States by any overall measure has been a good world citizen and has provided many kinds of assistance to other nations, there seems to be no historical balance sheet of international behavior by which people in other counties weigh past contributions of the United States against their current grievances.

The study focused on teenagers because "*they are the ones who are trained and equipped to conduct terrorists acts.* When examining the nature of such threats, and who it is that carries out actual terrorist activities, either in the U.S. or in other countries, one fact becomes very obvious. They are the young. Many Americans have seen televised scenes of youngsters as young as 12 being trained in terrorists' camps to engage in aggression against the infidel [read Americans]."

Few of those surveyed had any direct contact with Americans; only 12 percent had visited the U.S. But they did have access to American television programs, movies, and pop music. Based on that exposure, teenagers in these countries believe that Americans are generally quite violent; many American women are sexually immoral; Americans are very materialistic; Americans like to dominate other people; many Americans engage in criminal activities.

"These results suggest that pop culture, rather than foreign policy, is the true culprit of anti-Americanism," Melvin DeFleur says. "Hollywood should at least be asked by our public leaders to accept responsibility for the damage it is doing."[15]

Of course, the media is not the whole problem, but only one part of the equation—summed up in 1 Corinthians 15:33: "Do not be deceived: 'Bad company ruins good morals.'" This is the message of the Surgeon General's Report released on youth violence: Bad company corrupts good character, whether that bad company is gangs, peer pressure, or violent mass media of entertainment. Your children and teenagers are being affected by the bad company in the entertainment industry, even if it's only their friends or peers who are making bad entertainment choices.

When discussing media influence, we must also note that there is a lot of good programming out there, which we honor every March at the *Movieguide®* Annual Faith and Values Awards Gala and Report to the Entertainment Industry in Los Angeles. Since we started the event ten years ago, the number of movies with worthwhile moral, redemptive, and even Christian content has more than tripled! We can alert you and your family to the better and best movies and television programs—movies such as *Toy Story II, Monsters, Inc., The Rookie, The Princess Diaries, My Big Fat Greek Wedding, Evelyn, On the Line, Return to Me, Finding Nemo, Remember the Titans, Spider-Man, Nicholas Nickleby, My Dog Skip, Gods and Generals, Shrek, Joshua, Signs, We Were Soldiers, Chicken Run, Jimmy Neutron: Boy Genius*, and *The Basket*, and TV series like *Touched by an Angel, Jag, Doc*, and *7ᵗʰ Heaven*.

## YOUR CHILD'S COGNITIVE DEVELOPMENT

The second pillar in media wisdom is understanding the susceptibility of children at each stage of cognitive development. Not only do children see the media differently at each stage of their young lives, but also different children are susceptible to different stimuli. For instance, you might not want your younger children seeing *Spider-Man, Monsters, Inc., Shrek, Evelyn*, or The Lord of the Rings movies, while *Toy Story II, Stuart Little 2, Jimmy Neutron: Boy Genius*, and the Spy Kids movies are safer for them. Or you might want your teenager to avoid a movie like *The Family Man* or *We Were Soldiers*, but allow them to see something like *The Princess Diaries, Return to Me, The Lord of the Rings: The Return of the King, Evelyn, Nicholas Nickleby*, or *Minority Report*. As the research of the National Institute of Mental Health showed many years ago, some children want to copy media violence, some are susceptible to other media influences, some become afraid, and many simply become desensitized. Just as an alcoholic would be inordinately tempted by a beer commercial, so the child's susceptibility determines what kind of media will influence him or her at each stage of development.

# HOW THE ENTERTAINMENT MEDIA FUNCTIONS—ITS NATURE AND GRAMMAR

The third pillar of media wisdom is understanding the nature, politics, economics—the inner workings—of the media so that you can deconstruct and critique what you are watching. Children spend the first fourteen years of their lives learning grammar with respect to sixteenth-century technology—the written word. They need to be taught the rules of our twenty-first-century technology. They should know how aspects of different media work and influence them.

Children should be able to ask the right questions: Who is the hero? What kind of role model is the hero? Who is the villain? What message does his or her character convey? How much sex and violence is in the mass media product? What is the premise, or proposition, that drives the narrative? What worldview and values is the movie or program teaching? How does the movie or program treat Christians, Jews, religion, and political ideologies such as conservatism, liberalism, socialism, fascism, Marxism, or environmentalism? Does good triumph over evil? Would you be embarrassed to sit through this movie or television program with your parents, children, or Jesus Christ?

While the media present different types of stories, many of these stories contain recurrent universal and transcendent patterns, motifs, images, symbols, character types, themes, values, and principles. The recurring themes and character types are found in stories all over the world and throughout history. There is the task or the quest: A person or group of people must complete some great duty, such as Frodo's task to keep the ring hidden until he can destroy it properly. There is also the hero who always resolves the conflict. Then there are symbols, such as water, representing life, cleansing. These themes, symbols, and characters are often called archetypes. Archetypes are fundamental patterns or blueprints from which copies are made.

Some kinds of stories are more visually oriented, and other stories are more literary or theatrical. Also most stories embody the cultural ideals of a people and their society and give expression to deep, commonly felt, even transcendent emotions and rational or irrational ideas. Every story also has a worldview, a way of viewing reality, truth, the universe, the human condition, and the supernatural world. The theology of the storyteller helps shape the worldview of the story. Thus every worldview has a doctrine of God, a doctrine of man, a doctrine of salvation, a doctrine of the church, a doctrine of history and the future, a doctrine of the nature of reality (including a doctrine of nature or creation and a doctrine of supernatural forces), and a doctrine of knowledge (including a doctrine of truth).

The first two Harry Potter movies, for instance, have a New Age worldview that subtly encourages children to dabble in witchcraft and sorcery. The movies indirectly, and sometimes directly, teach a nature-based, gnostic, polytheistic religion that confuses the spiritual world of God with the natural or physical world, that has no doctrine of salvation or forgiveness for sin and believes human beings are basically good and not inherently sinful (as the Bible teaches). These films disdain the morality of the Christian church as well as the "Muggles" or ordinary people who make up that church. Further, they mock the belief in heaven and hell and in divine justice from a personal, rational God, and promote an epistemology or doctrine of knowledge that rejects rationality in favor of a belief in emotional decision-making and magical thinking.

In contrast to Harry Potter, The Lord of the Rings reflects the biblical, Christian understanding of reality. In Middle Earth there is a clear distinction between right and wrong and accountability. In Lord of the Rings, wielding vast supernatural power is seen as a temptation that should be shunned. The Lord of the Rings also provides the family with characters they can emulate, characters like Gandalf the Gray, the kindly supernatural being who dispenses wisdom, not unlike God, and has a good sense of humor. Then there is the character of Frodo himself, who humbly takes up the cross of "ring-bearer" so that he can keep the forces of darkness from gaining awesome power.

So how does the industry that churns out our films actually work? A quick tour of Hollywood provides some answers. The entertainment industry is made up of seven major studios and many independents. The major studios consistently control 95 percent or more of the box office and most of the other mass media of entertainment. The seven major studios also control the Motion Picture Association of America (MPAA), which rates the movies according to age groups—G, PG, PG-13, R, and NC-17. Because of their control, the past few years have seen an increase in PG-13 and R ratings so that greater amounts of explicit sex, nudity, violence, foul language, vulgarity, and other immorality can be marketed to your children and teenagers.

Those seven studios are run by executives who administrate, finance, and distribute movies. Keep in mind that the industry is made up of a small number of key players, but their decisions affect not only the United States but the world as well, because many areas of the world have come under the influence of Hollywood and its picture of the American experience. Thus there are about thirty financial and studio people who can green-light movie projects and about 300 key players, who consist of executive producers as well as a few directors and actors, who can easily get movies made by the major studios.

Each idea for a movie, however, originates from an executive producer (and/or a production company that could have deals going with several studios). In a sense, each movie is an independent unit that is brought together by an executive producer, who attaches to the project the director and stars and seeks financing from investors as well as the studios. The studio's major role is that of distribution—getting prints to the theaters and doing the publicity to bring in the audiences. Production and distribution budgets for major movies now average more than $89 million, according to the Motion Picture Association of America. One movie in 2000 had a $250 million cross-marketing budget, as reported by the *Los Angeles Times*.

An executive producer initiates each movie project. The movie starts with the story idea and the script. Sometimes writers are commissioned to write a script from an idea that a producer has, but often the writers create scripts they would like to have produced and "pitch" the idea to the producers. The director takes the script and the budget and, working with the actors and his crew, turns the idea into a reality on celluloid. In many cases the director is a hired hand, but often a director will also be a writer and producer.

## YOUR MORAL AND SPIRITUAL VALUES AND HOW TO TEACH THEM TO YOUR CHILDREN

Finally, the fourth pillar of media wisdom is to teach your children to understand your values and be able to use those values to evaluate the answers they get from asking the right questions. If the hero wins by murdering and mutilating, your children need to apply your own values, which will not see the hero's actions as heroic or commendable. Families have an easier time with this pillar of media wisdom because they can apply their deeply held religious beliefs to evaluate the media. Even so, media literacy and values education are two of the fastest growing areas in the academic community because educators realize that something is amiss.

Therefore, Dr. Ted Baehr, as chairman of the Christian Film & Television Commission, speaks all around the world at national education associations and presents his deeply held Christian beliefs as the yardstick he uses to evaluate the questions that need to be asked. When he speaks to Christian groups, he trains and equips them to immerse themselves in a biblical worldview so that they can help themselves, their children, and their grandchildren to choose the good and reject the bad.

Of course, there is much more to teaching media wisdom. Reading to your children five minutes a day is a most effective tool, according to University of Wisconsin research. Many parents may want to think about reading the Bible to their children. As Jesus Christ said, quoting Deuteronomy 8:3 in the Hebrew Scriptures, "Man does not live by bread alone, but man lives by every word that comes from the mouth of the LORD." Having your children prepare their own rating system, and then having them use it is also helpful, as is asking your children to review the media they consume by writing up their answers to the right questions. For more information on this, get a copy of the book *The Media-Wise Family*, available at amazon.com or by calling toll free at 1-800-899-6684.

President Theodore Roosevelt said that if we educate a man's mind but not his heart, we have an educated barbarian. Media wisdom involves educating the heart so that it will make the right decisions, which means not just rejecting the bad but also choosing the good. Is your family choosing the good?

# VI

# CARING IS THE ONLY DARING

*But whoever causes one of these little ones who believe in me to sin, it would be better for him to have a great millstone fastened around his neck and to be drowned in the depth of the sea.*

MATTHEW 18:6

A few years back the evening news broadcast a story about a baby-sitter in Dallas, Texas, who had molested the baby she was supposed to protect. The parents, who had become suspicious of the sitter, installed a hidden camera in their living room. The evening news showed what the parents saw—the baby-sitter starting to undress in front of the baby. Then the camera cut away. The news anchors were horrified and wondered how the parents had failed to check this sitter's credentials. The news team closed by remarking that this type of abuse probably occurs more often than anyone knows.

They were right. There is one baby-sitter who is constantly abusing millions of our children. No one fires this baby-sitter or brings criminal charges against it, nor do many people try to rehabilitate it.

## CHILD ABUSE VIA THE SILVER SCREEN

Even the secular press understands the problem of exposing children to violent and improper television and movies. In an article in the *Los*

*Angeles Times,* James Scott Bell[1], a lawyer, writer, and novelist in Los Angeles, noted:

> The country was rightly repulsed at the videotape of Madelyne Toogood beating her 4-year-old child in an Indiana parking lot. We know such mistreatment can have a terrible effect on a child's mental health. But, how many Americans indulge in a worse form of abuse without a second thought? I'm talking about taking kids to the movies. The wrong movies.
>
> The other night I saw *Red Dragon*, the third installment in the Hannibal Lecter series starring Anthony Hopkins. When the bad guy (Ralph Fiennes) bites off the tongue of a screaming reporter, then stands up, mouth bloody, and spits out the offending organ, I squirmed in my seat. What I couldn't stop thinking about, however, was the little girl in the seat in front of me.
>
> She looked about 6-years-old. . . . Two hours of mayhem ensued. People stabbed, set on fire, tortured. Your average day at the office for serial killers. Every now and then I'd lean over and see the little girl with her eyes fixed to the screen.

No matter how much we condemn the mass media for influencing the behavior of our children, we must admit that there are several accomplices in this tragedy. They include churches that don't help parents learn how to teach their children discernment and parents who allow their children to watch television, go to movies, or surf the Internet without adequate supervision or training in the necessary discernment skills.

## SEEK UNDERSTANDING

Understanding why and how the mass media affect children is an extremely important step in protecting your children and helping them develop the necessary critical thinking skills and discernment.

Many scientists have argued that there is such a significant body of evidence on the connection between the content of the mass media and behavior, especially aggressive behavior, that researchers should move beyond accumulating further evidence and focus on the processes responsible for the behavior. According to Dr. Victor Strasburger, chief of The American Academy of Pediatrics' section on adolescents, "We are basically saying the controversy is over. There is clearly a relationship between media violence and violence in society."[2]

A report on four decades of entertainment TV from the media research team of Robert Lichter, Linda Lichter, Stanley Rothman, and Daniel Amundson found about fifty crimes, including a dozen murders, in every hour of prime time television. Our children may see from 800,000 to 1.5 million acts of violence and witness 192,000 to 360,000 murders on television by the time they are seventeen years old.[3]

What a contrast to the generations of men and women who grew up *without* this flood of violent images from the entertainment media. Lichter and his fellow authors wrote, "Since 1955 TV characters have been murdered at a rate 1,000 times higher than real-world victims."[4] If the same murder rate were applied to the general population, everyone in the United States would be killed in just fifty days.[5]

If you are over forty years old, you probably watch only six movies a year in theaters, most of which are family films. By comparison teenagers watch an average of fifty movies, 80 percent of which are R-rated or PG-13. They watch another fifty movies a year on video.[6]

## FIVE SEASONS

To know why children are affected by the mass media, we need first to understand how children develop mentally. For this information we turn to the field of psychology. It is important to note that psychology, including the field known as cognitive development, is descriptive in that it helps us to classify and understand human beings (after all, God gave man the job of naming what he saw). For many Christians, psychology falls short of being able to cure a problem that it identifies, whereas the Bible has the cure for what ails us.

It was the renowned child psychologist Jean Piaget[7] who identified the major stages of mental development through which children progress. In the late 1970s television researcher Robert Morse[8] adapted Piaget's stages so that they can be more effectively applied to research into the mass media.

Every child goes through the stages listed on the following pages. (Please note that the use of masculine pronouns throughout the following sections is simply for ease of grammatical transition and is not intended as exclusionary language. These stages and principles apply to girls as well as boys.)

• The sensation stage[9] (approximately ages birth to two years old) where the child's sole means of processing reality is his senses. These young children think that they are the center of the universe and that everything around them serves them. To them something exists only if they can see it.

• The imagination stage[10] (approximately ages two to seven years old) where the child acquires skills such as language, mental imagery, drawing, and symbolic play. During this stage the child has a very active imagination, often confusing fact and fiction, making him uniquely susceptible to what he sees on television and in movies. It is not surprising that a four-year-old girl was critically injured after she apparently tried to fly after watching the *Harry Potter and the Sorcerer's Stone* movie. Authorities in Shelby, North Carolina, said that the girl watched the movie and then crawled onto a kitchen counter, straddled a broom, and jumped off.

• The concrete operational stage (approximately ages seven to eleven years old) where the child acquires the ability of simultaneous perception of two points of view, enabling him to master quantities, relations, and classes of objects. At this stage there is a strong correspondence between the child's thoughts and reality. He assumes his thoughts about reality are accurate and distorts the facts to fit what he thinks. Younger children react to direct violence but not to suspense. Children in the concrete stage are more upset by suspense than by direct violence. Thus children in the earlier stages will be bored by *Jaws,* which is mostly suspense, while older children may be traumatized by it.

• The reflection or formal operations stage (approximately ages twelve to fifteen years old) where the child begins to do abstract thinking. In this stage the adolescent has not yet learned to conceptualize the thoughts of others. He assumes that other people are as obsessed with his behavior and appearance as he is. For example, if he has a pimple and walks into a room filled with friends, he will usually think that everyone is looking at his pimple. The young person in this stage will take risks because he still has difficulty recognizing the consequences of his actions. For instance, when the movie *The Program* was released, several teenagers mimicked the main characters by lying down in the middle of the road to prove their courage. Some of these teenagers were seriously injured, and some were killed.

One national radio personality said that these teenagers were really stupid. However, one of the teenagers who died was at the top of his class. What the radio personality did not understand was that these teenagers were in a stage of development when they were the most impulsive and the least able to consider the consequences of their actions. Also peer pressure and other factors may have influenced these teens' behavior.

• The relationship stage wherein the adolescent grows into a mature adult. The adult understands that others are different from himself and accepts those differences by learning to relate to others. Furthermore, the adult is able to recognize the consequences of his actions and take the necessary steps to reduce risks.

## BABES IN TOYLAND

When children watch horror films, they experience fear. They must find ways to cope with the emotions raised by the violence, particularly if they are exposed to large amounts of it. Coping often entails either desensitization or imitation.

Researchers Barbara J. Wilson, Daniel Lynn, and Barbara Randall have examined the harmful effects of graphic horror on children and discovered some important distinctions:[11]

• *Visual versus nonvisual threat.* Younger children are likely to be frightened by movies and television programs with *visually* frightening creatures such as witches and monsters. Older children will focus more on *nonvisual* qualities, such as the motives of a character,[12] and are likely to be more upset by an evil, normal-looking character or by an unseen threat than by a benign but grotesque character. Therefore, *The Wizard of Oz* is more frightening for younger children than for older children, while older children are more frightened by movies such as *Poltergeist* and *Jaws*, which rely on nonvisual threats.

• *Reality versus fantasy.* Younger children are unable to fully distinguish between reality and fantasy.[13] Although the terms "real" and "make-believe" may be used in conversation, younger children do not understand the implications of these terms. The notion that a character or an event is "not real" has little impact on a younger child's emotions. Therefore, fantasy events that could not possibly happen, such as in Harry Potter, are more frightening to younger children, whereas fictional events that could happen, such as in *Jaws*, are more frightening to older children and adults.[14]

• *Abstract versus concrete events*. A concrete threat is explicit and tangible. For example, an evil character might attack a victim. In contrast, abstract threats must be inferred from information in the plot. Examples might include movies about evil conspiracies or disasters caused by poisonous gases. Younger children have difficulty drawing inferences from entertainment and are more likely to focus on explicit rather than implicit cues in the plot.[15] So they will be more frightened by a movie depicting a concrete threat than one involving an intangible or obscure hazard.

• *Threat versus victim focus*. Also cognitive stages are distinguished by the degree to which the scenes concentrate on the actual threat versus the victim's emotional reactions to the threat. Movies that require viewer involvement and focus primarily on the victims' emotional reactions are less upsetting for younger than for older children. *Jaws* is a good example because the viewer often sees only the upper bodies of the victims as they are attacked by the unseen shark.

More important than the sheer amount of horror and violence children watch is the way in which even small amounts of violence are portrayed.[16] Therefore, a number of contextual features of violence are critical in determining whether aggressive behavior results.[17] According to Wilson, Lynn, and Randall, these contextual features are:

• *Reward versus punishment associated with violence*. When the aggressor is rewarded for violent behavior, children are most likely to imitate it or to develop aggressive attitudes.[18] In fact, characters need not be explicitly rewarded for such effects to occur. As long as there is no punishment for a violent act, young viewers will often imitate it.[19] The lack of punishment is a reward for such behavior. Much media violence is portrayed without negative consequences; neither perpetrators nor victims suffer much, and the perpetrator is often rewarded for antisocial actions, as in Harry Potter.[20]

The timing of the reward or punishment has important developmental implications.[21] In many movies the perpetrator receives material rewards immediately after performing an aggressive act. Punishment, however, is typically delivered toward the end of the movie. Since younger children are less able than older children to coherently link scenes together and to draw inferences from them,[22] younger children are more likely than older children to see the violence as acceptable and to imitate it, when rewards are immediate and punishment is delayed in a movie.

• *Degree of reality of violence.* Violence perceived to be realistic is more likely to be imitated and used as a guide for behavior.[23] Older children are better able to distinguish reality from fantasy and are more emotionally responsive to programs that depict realistic events. Thus, older children are affected more by violent movies that feature events that are humanly possible, such as *Scream.* Younger children are responsive to both realistic and unrealistic violence as long as the acts are concrete and visual.

• *The nature of the perpetrator.* Children are more likely to imitate models who are attractive or interesting.[24] Children who strongly identify with violent media characters are more likely to be aggressive themselves than are those who do not identify with such characters.[25]

Younger children are more likely to focus on the consequences of a character's behavior in determining whether the character is "good" or "bad," whereas older children focus more on the character's motives.[26] These age differences are probably due to the fact that motives are usually presented early in a plot so that the viewer is able to draw inferences in order to link them to subsequent behaviors. Therefore, younger children will be more likely to emulate bad characters as long as they are rewarded, whereas older children, in selecting role models, may take into account the characters' motives.

• *Justified violence.* Violence portrayed as justified is more likely to be imitated.[27] A common theme in many movies is a hero who is forced to be violent because his job demands it (e.g., *Dirty Harry*) or because he has to retaliate against an enemy (e.g., Harry Potter). Even though the ultimate message may promote the good of society (e.g., don't be a criminal), the moral is conveyed in a violent context. The violence easily overwhelms the social good.

In one experiment examining "mixed messages,"[28] children viewed either a cartoon with a good message in a nonviolent context or a cartoon with a good message delivered through justified violence. Kindergartners were more likely to hurt than to help a peer after watching the aggressive cartoon. Moreover, both younger and older children showed less understanding of the moral lesson when it was conveyed in the context of violence. A hero who commits violence for some "good" cause is likely to be a confusing and negative role model for all children.

• *Similarity of movie situations and characters to reality.* Viewers are more likely to imitate media violence if cues in the program are similar to those in real life.[29] Also children are likely to imitate models who are similar to themselves.[30] Thus movies depicting children as violent are more problematic than those involving violent adults. Preschool and early elementary school children focus on younger characters who are violent, whereas preteens and teenagers attend more to aggressive teenage characters.

• *Amount of violence.* Although the *way* violence is portrayed is more critical than the *amount* of violence when it comes to aggressive behavior, the sheer amount and explicitness of the violent content has a critical impact on the viewer's emotions. Excessive exposure to violence may "psychologically blunt" normal emotional responses to violent events. Heavy viewers of television violence show less physiological arousal to a clip of filmed violence than light viewers.

In one experiment children who watched a violent film or television program were afterward less likely to seek help when the other children became disruptive and violent. Thus exposure to media violence leads to a lack of responsiveness to real-life aggression.[31]

## DANGEROUS MINDS

Part of the problem with television as well as movies is that they are so effective at propelling powerful, emotional images into the viewer's mind in real time with no chance to reflect, react, or review the information— processes absolutely necessary for cognitive development.

The very act of watching is harmful to the cognitive development of children and, as a result, adversely affects their moral, social, emotional, and religious development as well. But children are not the only ones affected. Watching most videos and television impairs "an important cognitive function in adults, the one that permits abstract reasoning—and hence related capacities for moral decision making, learning, religious growth, and psychological individualization."[32]

## RUSH

Watching fighting or other violence can make the mind believe that it is about to engage in life-threatening activity. The body will often respond by releasing adrenal epinephrine into the bloodstream, giving the viewer an adrenal rush without the threat of actual violence. Watching sexual activity and nudity makes the mind think that the person is about to mate; so the body releases raging hormones that can often cause an addictive adrenal rush without the psychological burdens that come with most human relationships. These physiological phenomena will engage and attract the viewer, often causing him or her to want more and more exposure to the stimuli that cause their artificial physical elation.

Scientists have discovered that mass media violence leads to aggressive behavior by overstimulating children. The more intense and realistic the violent scene, the more likely it is to be encoded, stored in the memory, and later retrieved as model behavior.

Another study showed that boys who watch a great deal of violent programming may exhibit less physiological arousal when shown new violent programs than do boys who regularly watch less violent fare.[33] This study seems to explain why consumers of mass media sex and violence need more and more prurient or violent fare. Of course, all of this can add up to addiction (best summed up by the phrase the "plug-in drug," as applied to television) because most of the offerings of the mass media are emotional, not intellectual pursuits.

The impact of excessive movie and television sex and violence on teenagers is aggravated by the fact that their raging hormones give them a predisposition to seek arousal. They are subject to tremendous peer and media pressure at an age when fitting in with their peers is extremely important even if that fitting in means rebelling against their parents. They have a predisposition to seek out movies and programs that arouse them. Some are so aroused they seek to replicate the sexual or violent situations portrayed in the movie or television program in their own lives.

## TRUTH OR CONSEQUENCES

Part of the reason for the breakdown of morality in movies and television today, and in the culture at large, is that people of faith retreated from being salt and light in the culture. From 1933 to 1966 they were a predominant force in Hollywood. During that period, the Roman Catholic Legion of Decency and the Protestant Film Commission (which started several years after the Legion of Decency) read every script to ensure that movies attracted the largest possible audience by adhering to high standards of decency.

It took ten years and God's grace acting through several dedicated Christian men to position God's people to be such a powerful moral influence on Hollywood. Prior to their involvement in 1933, American movies were morally bankrupt—full of nudity, perversity, and violence. From 1922 to 1933, church-going men and women tried everything, including censorship boards, to influence Hollywood to make wholesome entertainment. Nothing succeeded until people of faith volunteered to work alongside the Hollywood studios to help them reach the largest possible audience, a strategy being used successfully today at the Christian Film & Television Commission ministry and *Movieguide®*.

When the Protestant Film Office closed its advocacy offices in Hollywood in 1966 (in spite of many pleas to stay by the top Hollywood filmmakers), not only did it open the floodgates to violence (*The Wild Bunch*), sex and Satanism (*Rosemary's Baby*), and perverse anti-religious bigotry (*Midnight Cowboy*), it also caused a severe drop in movie attendance from forty-four million tickets sold per week to about twenty million.

Since the church abandoned Hollywood, violent crime has increased in the United States by 560 percent; illegitimate births have increased 419 percent; divorces rates have quadrupled; the percentage of children living in single-parent homes has tripled; the teenage suicide rate has increased more than 300 percent; SAT scores have dropped almost 80 points. Rapes, murders, and gang violence have become common occurrences. While many factors have contributed to our cultural decline, it is clear that the mass media has had a significant influence on behavior.[34]

Researchers affiliated with the National Bureau of Economic

Research and Stanford University wrote in the journal *Science*[35] that America's children are fatter, more suicidal, more murderous, and scored lower on standardized tests in recent years than in the 1960s. After years of denial, even 87 percent of the top media executives now admit that the violence in the mass media contribute to the violence in society.[36] And children too are aware, in a limited way, of the ability of the entertainment media to influence their behavior.[37]

Yet in spite of the clear correlation between violence in the mass media and violence on the street, very few people are yelling "Stop!" The growing American tolerance for brutal media sex and violence suggests the proverbial frog who calmly dies as he is slowly brought to a boil.

The apostle Paul's letter to the Romans describes the conditions in which we find ourselves today:

> *And since they did not see fit to acknowledge God, God gave them up to a debased mind to do what ought not to be done. They were filled with all manner of unrighteousness, evil, covetousness, malice. They are full of envy, murder, strife, deceit, maliciousness. They are gossips, slanderers, haters of God, insolent, haughty, boastful, inventors of evil, disobedient to parents, foolish, faithless, heartless, ruthless. Though they know God's decree that those who practice such things deserve to die, they not only do them but give approval to those who practice them. (Romans 1:28-32)*

## A SAMPLE OF THE VIOLENCE

The suggestion that the mass media of entertainment spawns violence is not anecdotal; it is real. Over the years have come innumerable reports of grisly crimes inspired by films. These stories help us realize the scope of the problem and the powerful influence of movies, television programs, music, and the other mass media. A small sampling of specific films and their violent outcomes is outlined below.

### Glorifying Gangs

Gang movies have left a trail of tears and death. Police have called some of these films "irresponsible" and "exploitive." At the opening of filmmaker John Singleton's movie *Boyz in the Hood*, thirty-three people were injured in a fight that broke out, and two died from gunshot wounds. When this movie was shown in one California prison, fourteen people died in one night of race rioting in the prison.

When *New Jack City* opened, riots broke out in Los Angeles, New York, Chicago, and Houston. More than 1,500 teenagers rampaged through Westwood, Los Angeles. A teenager was killed in Brooklyn where rival gangs fired more than 100 shots.

## Child's Play?

It is clear to any parent that children learn to a large degree by mimicking the behavior of the adults around them, including those on television and in movies.[38] One of the most famous examples was the connection that a judge in Liverpool, England, made between the horror movie *Child's Play 3* and the murder of two-year-old James Bulger by two eleven-year-old boys, Robert Thompson and Jon Venables.[39] According to the judge, this movie presents some horrifying parallels to the actual murder of the little boy, and the movie was viewed repeatedly by one of the killers just before the murder took place. The judge noted:

• The horror movie depicts a baby doll who comes to life and gets blue paint splashed in its face. There was blue paint on the dead child's face.

• The movie depicts a kidnapping. James was abducted by the two older boys before they killed him.

• The climax of the movie comes as two young boys murder the doll on a train, mutilating the doll's face. James was first mutilated and bludgeoned by the two older boys and then left on a railroad track to be run over.

This story was widely publicized around the world, but the link to *Child's Play 3* seldom made the news. Why were these facts overlooked or withheld by the mainstream media?

## Slasher Movies

Thirteen-year-old Eric Smith lured four-year-old Derrick Robie into the woods, bludgeoned his head with rocks, and sodomized the body. According to press reports about the crime, Eric loved reading Stephen King novels and watching gruesome slasher movies—the more pornographic, the better. Jurors found Eric Smith guilty of second-degree murder.

In Houston, Texas, Scott Edward May, a seventeen-year-old obsessed with slasher movies and occult and heavy-metal music, attacked a girl during their first date, stabbing her when she closed her eyes for a good night kiss.[40] They had just seen the movie *The Cutting Edge*. May told police he had had urges to kill since childhood. "I love knives," May's statement reads. "I like to go to the movies a lot. A lot of people get stabbed in the movies. I really liked *Texas Chainsaw Massacre*. A lot of people got stabbed in that."

### Natural Born Killers?

The Oliver Stone movie *Natural Born Killers* has produced a slew of copycat murders. Nathan K. Martinez, an unhappy seventeen-year-old obsessed with this movie, murdered his stepmother and his half-sister in their suburban home fifteen miles southwest of Salt Lake City. In Georgia fifteen-year-old Jason Lewis murdered his parents, firing multiple shotgun blasts into their heads. Letters found in his room indicated he worshiped Satan and, along with three friends, had made plans to kill all their parents and to copy the cross-country swing of violence portrayed in *Natural Born Killers*. Eighteen-year-old Christopher Smith shouted at television cameras, "I'm a natural born killer!" echoing the words of actor Woody Harrelson in the movie following his arrest for shooting an eighty-two-year-old man to death.

One gruesome incident prompted novelist John Grisham to suggest that the survivors of these killing sprees should sue Stone.[41] In March 1995 two teenagers saw *Natural Born Killers* in Oklahoma and then drove to Mississippi and killed Bill Savage in the same randomly violent way as the movie's protagonists. They then went to Louisiana and nearly killed a women in a convenience store (she is now a quadriplegic). One of the two said the movie led directly to their actions.

## WHAT ELSE?

Increased violence in our society would be more than enough, but it is not the only effect of the mass media of entertainment on children. This fare kills creative imagination and hinders the ability to concentrate and to delay gratification. Young media consumers can develop false memory syndrome. Many make an idol of movies/TV and serve it with religious devotion. Some are drawn into spiritual warfare and even open their souls to evil spirits.

## The Twilight Zone

Heavy users of mass media of entertainment are less able to form "mental pictures," and they engage in less imaginative play than other children. Heavy consumers become lazy readers of "nonbooks." They have greatly decreased attention spans (you have to exercise concentration, or it atrophies). These children have less tolerance for getting into a book or other activities.

The child's ability to symbolize, perceive, and do abstract reasoning are damaged in a manner that resembles dyslexia. The rapid increase in reading disabilities, or dyslexia, in the United States may be in part attributed to heavy television and movie viewing. Television in particular inhibits eye movement, making it more difficult for a child to acquire reading skills.

## False Memory Syndrome

The whole area of false memory syndrome, unchained memories, memory therapy, and associated psychological insights has captured the national imagination. A tremendous amount of movie and television sex, violence, and occultism has filled the minds of youth over the years. Nefarious films and other mass media have planted images in their minds that they have processed in the same manner as the daily activities in which they engage. However, unlike the many daily activities that are repetitive and dull, most of these entertaining movies and television programs are a potent and often traumatic brew of visual and audio messages that lodge in the nooks and crannies of the child's memory, waiting to pop into their dreams or consciousness.

Research indicates that the minds of our youth are overflowing with images from movies and television programs that they confuse with reality and history. Everyday examples abound. One woman who saw the movie *Independence Day* afterwards told a reporter that she believes the government is hiding a flying saucer. Some, including a media literacy teacher who saw the movie *The Wind and the Lion,* assume that this historical incident involved a beautiful woman and a dashing desert chieftain, rather than the real characters—an old Greek immigrant and a Moroccan thief.

Memory therapists have been able to induce adults to fabricate a childhood history from disjointed memories. Regrettably, some of these adults have acted upon these false memories.

### God Rewritten Hollywood-Style

The mass media affect not only our behavior but also our beliefs. Religion is alive and well in the mass media, though it is not the predominantly Christian faith of our founding fathers. The mass media religion is instead a concoction of materialism, consumerism, eroticism, hedonism, naturalism, humanism, cynicism, stoicism, the cult of violence, and a multitude of other modern variations on pagan practices that now vie for renewed homage.

Dr. Kathleen Waller and Dr. Michael E. O'Keeffe team-teach the popular "Religion and Film" course at Saint Xavier University in Chicago. They note that movies deeply influence how their students see God and theology. They wrote in *Movieguide®*:

> We have come to two conclusions about our students that give us pause. The first is the relative insecurity many of our students feel when explaining their faith; and the second is the undeniable influence that the mass media has on the religious ideas they do hold. . . .
>
> These students certainly consider themselves good Christians, but they lack the ability to discuss their faith with anything more than a surface understanding of who Jesus is and what Christianity is about. In short, they are unable to "explain" their views, particularly to classmates who come from religious traditions that do not use the same terms or speak from the starting point they do. Thus even discussing something as seemingly straightforward as "the Bible is the Word of God" is difficult for them, particularly if they are called upon to explain the theological presuppositions that stand behind such a claim.
>
> Perhaps because of this naïveté, many of our students also struggle with the second fact; namely, their almost wholesale acceptance of the culture's understanding of religion. In other words, they are relatively uniformed about the faith given to them by their parents and their

churches, and they are uninformed about the distinction between that faith and the "faith" packaged for them by the mass media, especially films and television. Hence our task is doubled: we not only have to help students sort out and explain the inherited faith of our fathers and mothers, but we have to distinguish true faith from the faith of Hollywood. In many cases, the faith of our students is more indebted to *The Simpsons* and movies such as *Stigmata* and *Dogma* than to traditional Christianity.

. . . Our experience confirms it is more difficult to dislodge Hollywood's version of Christianity, for Hollywood's version eventually becomes "real," becomes the way they see God, or heaven and hell, or sin and virtue, or the lives of believers vis-à-vis the lives of others.

The themes portrayed are consistent: malevolent supernatural forces are real, humans are powerless in the face of evil, Christian doctrine and religious training provide no recourse or significant spiritual guidance in the struggle with evil, and the Christian Church and its leaders are powerless before Satan and his minions. In addition, God is too distant, or uncaring, unable, or unwilling to check Satan's power. These films, and others like them, borrow freely from Christian teachings and symbols, but usually subvert them beyond recognition or take such dramatic license that any sound theological insight is lost. They often purport to quote from the Bible or to interpret biblical eschatology, but these interpretations are horribly skewed at best. Several of the movies are visually stunning in their special effects; so, even if one is able to recognize the faulty theology, the world they portray is so compelling that it is hard not to accept Hollywood's version as true. Thus it is not surprising that many of our students are unable to distinguish the unorthodox teaching in these films. Instead, they come away convinced they have learned something valuable about Christianity and its inability to deal with evil.[42]

As theologian Paul Tillich explains, "Your god is that reality which elicits from you your deepest feelings and ultimate concerns," and "religion is the state of being grasped by an ultimate concern, a concern which qualifies all other concerns as preliminary and which itself contains the answer to the question of a meaning of our life."[43] British playwright J. M. Barrie states that "one's religion is whatever he is most interested in."[44]

The Internet, computer games, prime time entertainment television, movies, and popular music have become a religion for too many, especially some of those employed in the entertainment industry.

Unfortunately, children have lost all memory of the Ten Commandments with the prohibitions against murder, theft, and adultery, among the other absolute moral values, as illustrated by the following chart:

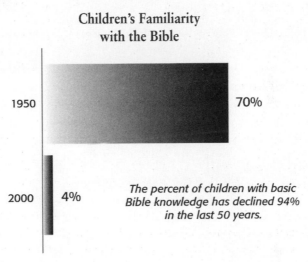

### Children's Familiarity with the Bible

1950          70%

2000    4%     *The percent of children with basic Bible knowledge has declined 94% in the last 50 years.*

### Spiritual Warfare

The mass media also has a spiritual impact. Its images tug at our desires, seduce our thoughts, and lodge in our memories. They claw at our consciousness and entice us to do things we would not otherwise do, whether to buy a product we don't need or worse. These images are the demons of our age.

We often forget that a war rages around us. It is a war being waged inside our minds, a spiritual war for our souls. The Adversary is using every possible tactic to control our minds: materialism, secularism, humanism, and all the other isms that conflict with Christianity. He is using the most effective weapons to win—the power of the mass media of entertainment. With the corrupted movies and television programs of our age, he fuels our sinful propensity to lust and hooks us on our desires. Once we are hooked, he drags us down to hell.

### Seducing Spirits

In *Seductions Exposed*, Gary Greenwald suggests that there is a danger of what he terms the "transference of spirits."[45] If we are in Christ Jesus, we cannot be possessed by any spirit other than the Holy Spirit of God, but we can be oppressed, enticed, and deceived.

Greenwald contends that some of the avenues in which transference of spirits can occur include movies, television, music, and magazines that contain violence, pornography, lust, and immorality. Thus the Adversary has enslaved millions with the spirit of this world through their eyes and ears.

Because sin is seductive, Greenwald notes, we can be slowly affected by the devil without even realizing that our attitudes have changed. Thus, the sexual immorality and profanity on television and in movies that once shocked us, no longer disturb us once we grow accustomed to them. However, when it is too late, we find that we have been trapped.

The ultimate trial that we face if we have allowed ourselves to be seduced by the spirits of our age is that "we must all appear before the judgment seat of Christ, so that each one may receive what is due for what he has done in the body, whether good or evil" (2 Corinthians 5:10). As the apostle Paul notes in 1 Corinthians 15:33: "Do not be deceived: 'Bad company ruins good morals.'"

## A SHORTCUT IS THE LONGEST DISTANCE

The information contained in this chapter is no doubt overwhelming to many parents. The statistics and stories seem impossible to overcome. There is no shortcut to becoming media-wise, but you have taken a crucial first step in becoming informed about the influence the entertainment media has on our society, particularly with regard to violence, sexual activity, and values. From this foundation, you can learn to develop discernment and biblical critical thinking skills regarding such influence. Children, in particular, are motivated to change their media habits by an awareness of the influence of the entertainment media on these areas of their lives. Once they understand the power of the mass media to negatively influence them, they will become your ally in the culture wars. They will want to develop media awareness, discernment, and the critical thinking skills necessary to choose the good, reject the bad, and overcome the negative images.

On the positive side of the influence of the entertainment media equation, the epic television program *Jesus of Nazareth* introduced millions of people throughout the world to Jesus Christ; *A Man Called Peter*, about the preacher Peter Marshall, brought a flood of many young men into church pulpits; *Chariots of Fire* brought many to Jesus and gave many more a sense of God's purpose in their life.

The key is for Christians and the church to develop wisdom, knowledge, understanding, and discernment by rediscovering and recapturing a biblical theology of art, entertainment, and communication. Thus equipped, it becomes much easier to comprehend and choose between Harry Potter and The Lord of the Rings.

# VII

# ONCE UPON A TIME: WORLDVIEWS, FANTASY, MYTH, AND BEYOND

*In the beginning was the Word, and the Word was with God, and the Word was God. He was in the beginning with God. All things were made through him, and without him was not any thing made that was made. In him was life, and the life was the light of men. The light shines in the darkness, and the darkness has not overcome it. . . . The Word became flesh and dwelt among us, and we have seen his glory, glory as of the only Son from the Father, full of grace and truth.*

JOHN 1:1-5, 14

This, of course, is the poetic, profound opening passage to the Gospel of John, one of the apostles of Jesus Christ. This passage tells an important story about the real identity of Jesus Christ, the Son of God who was sent by God the Father and who died for our sins so that we may have eternal life.

Many people have called this Christ story "the greatest story ever told." As such, it provides an archetypal pattern for all stories, as noted by Stan Williams in "Popular Motion Pictures Are Imbued with the Center of All Truth."[1] Most successful motion pictures follow a typical three-act structure of setup, confrontation, and resolution, which can include at least two plot points, including the promise of a new opportunity and a major setback.

"The first turning point," writes Dr. Williams, "is really the *birth* of the protagonist's new identity that allows him to pursue his goal. That new identity is confronted and tested throughout Act 2, resulting in the protagonist's sustained *suffering*. The turning point between Act 2 and Act 3 usually involves a major *sacrifice* by the protagonist or someone close to him. This leads to Act 3 where the protagonist experiences *redemption* of his identity and attainment of his goal."[2]

This structure of promise, birth, suffering, sacrifice, and redemption is the story of the gospel of Jesus Christ, Dr. Williams believes. The promise of the coming Messiah, predicted in the Hebrew Scriptures, is fulfilled by the birth of Jesus Christ in the New Testament. The birth of Christ provides a "new opportunity for the relationship between God and mankind," Dr. Williams notes.[3] In Act 2, however, Jesus Christ suffers and must sacrifice his life. Finally, in Act 3, "Christ is resurrected and achieves the goal promised from the beginning—mankind's redemption."[4]

This Christ-motif can be found in many recent popular movies, including the first Lord of the Rings movie, *The Fellowship of the Ring*. In this film Gandalf offers his own life so that the Fellowship may continue on its journey to destroy the evil magic ring and defeat the satanic forces trying to take complete control of Middle Earth. You can even find the motif in the second Harry Potter movie and book, where Harry Potter sacrifices himself but must undergo a kind of resurrection at the end so that he can free Dobby, the house elf, from slavery to the evil Malfoy patriarch.

As Dr. Williams wisely cautions, "Although the Gospel structure is inherently present, the explicit story and message of a motion picture can be distorted. So, when men of ominous intent control the storytelling process, we hear stories and get messages about gratuitous evil."[5]

Thus although there may be redemptive qualities in the Harry Potter series of books and movies, there are also strong negative qualities. Harry Potter uses evil means—lying, seeking revenge, disobedience, and, worst of all, various forms of sorcery or witchcraft—to achieve his goals. As such, Harry Potter presents an immoral worldview that explicitly contradicts the biblical, Christian worldview of the Hebrew Scriptures and the New Testament documents. This is why it is extremely important for families to know how the worldviews and stories in movies, videos, and television programs are structured and how they can affect cognitive, moral, and spiritual development.

## WORLDVIEWS EXPLAINED

What is a worldview? According to Norman Geisler and William Watkins in *Worlds Apart: A Handbook of World Views*, a worldview is "a way of viewing or interpreting all of reality."[6] Later they add that a worldview provides "an interpretive framework through which or by which one makes sense out of the data of life and the world."[7] All comprehensive worldviews seem to share at least five things: 1) They have a cosmology—a view of the "physical" or "material" universe; 2) They have a metaphysics—a view of what might or might not exist beyond the universe; 3) They have an anthropology—a view of human beings and their environment and culture; 4) They have a psychology—a view of the human soul and the mental, emotional, spiritual, and interior life of human beings; and, 5) They have an axiology—a philosophy of values.

In general, a good worldview must have at least three things—internal consistency, explanatory power, and adequacy or sufficiency. Thus it must be logical, it must be able to explain many different kinds of phenomenon, and it must fit the facts.

How many different worldviews are there?

Scholars categorize worldviews in varying ways. The Christian Film & Television Commission's flagship publication *Movieguide®* identifies six basic worldviews. Four of these are explicitly and often implicitly anti-Christian and anti-biblical.

### Nihilism

In this view everything is meaningless. The possibility of any objective truth or knowledge is denied. Nihilism asserts that the universe is without purpose, that human life lacks any value and significance, and that moral values are totally arbitrary. Under nihilism, all choices are meaningless, and hence all choices are objectively and morally equivalent.

## Humanism

This view holds that man is the measure of all things; however, modern humanism is not just a man-centered system. Accepting (as a matter of good faith) the definition of humanism in *The Humanist Manifesto*, modern humanism (unlike traditional or Christian humanism, which examined man in a biblical context) believes that only the material world exists. There is no supernatural or nonmaterial world, no God, no gods, and usually no alien "others." Man has no soul. He is just a meat machine that has "evolved" according to some form of Darwinism. Modern humanism always has a strong anti-supernatural bias. Marx said that his communism was the ultimate humanism and advocated that a humanist society should abolish religion, the family, the nation, and private property.

## Romanticism

This view is not related to the idea of romance but is an idealistic world-view. Man is essentially good and noble, and civilization (by which Rousseau, the father of Romantic philosophy, meant Christianity) corrupts man. Man is controlled by his heart and emotions, not by his intellect or logical mind. Romanticism turned away from Christianity and prompted the investigation of the occult and a return to pre-Christian pagan practices. The Romantic philosophy is credited with inspiring the Reign of Terror of the French Revolution, Marxism, and the Nazi movement in Germany. Thus paganism and mob rule are related to Romanticism, though Romanticism is more consistent.

## Paganism

Eclectic, "anything goes" worship of whatever gods anyone desires to worship characterizes this view. Paganism has a nontraditional belief system (or a mixture of belief systems), without Christian or biblical values. Sensual pleasures and material goods are often, but not always, the main goal in life. Often paganism leads to hedonism, anarchy, or a fascist dictatorship. This view involves spiritism, use of magic, or worship of many false gods, with one of the gods sometimes being singled out for special worship or particular lifelong devotion. Paganism also includes what is sometimes called New Age thought with its roots in gnosticism, Buddhism, and Hinduism. Gnosticism counterfeits Christianity and proposes that one needs special, secret knowledge to overcome the evil world in which people live and so to ascend into the true "divine" reality.

## Moral Worldview and the Christian Worldview

These two worldviews carry positive connotations. They are separated because many movies are not explicitly or even implicitly Christian, but they may contain moral or biblical elements, including references to the moral principles described by Moses in the Hebrew Scriptures and/or by Jesus Christ and his disciples in the New Testament, references to the historical figures in the Bible, or references to the characters in the parables of Jesus Christ. The Christian worldview, of course, implies that people are sinful and in need of redemption. Thus a Christian worldview values such things as repentance, forgiveness, sacrifice, and service. It also makes explicit and implicit references to the gospel of Jesus Christ, including the death, resurrection, and vicarious atonement of Jesus Christ, as well as references to the kingdom of God that Christ came to establish in the hearts and lives of human beings.

Christianity, a form of ethical monotheism, is superior to all of the non-Christian or anti-Christian worldviews because it is logical, it explains many different kinds of phenomenon, and it fits the facts.

The Christian worldview affirms the existence of an ordered, physical universe created by an eternal, transcendental, personal God, who is inherently benevolent, loving, and thoughtful. This God has instilled in people the ability to engage in rational or logical thought and empirical observation, as when a historian, scientist, theologian, or film critic rationally examines factual evidence. Thus, the Christian worldview affirms the general validity but not the infallibility of science, history, theology, and film criticism.

The Christian worldview also accepts the idea that truth exists and can be known by finite, or limited, human beings. This truth is objective, transcendent, and absolute because God and his existence are objective, transcendent, and absolute. It is perfectly proper, therefore, for human beings to spend their lives searching for objective, transcendent, absolute truth.

The Christian worldview proclaims that there is an objective, transcendent moral order (or set of essential moral values and principles)
that every person must obey. These moral values and principles are part
of God's character. Thus, in this way, Christianity provides a rational
justification for judging what is good or evil, right or wrong, true or
false, and proper or improper. Without a worldview such as Christian
theism, we could not claim that murder is wrong or that going to war
against Nazi Germany in World War II was the right thing to do.
Because of all this, the Christian worldview has an intellectually and
emotionally compelling moral philosophy.

The Christian worldview is also superior because it gives human
beings a meaningful love. The love that God has for human beings is
rooted in the loving, transcendent, eternal relationship that exists
between the Father, the Son, and the Holy Spirit, the three persons who
make up the one true God. This "trinity" is not an irrational concept
because the three persons in the Godhead share the single divine substance, divine nature, and divine being of the one true God.

Perhaps most importantly, the Christian worldview, because it is
based on a set of historical documents (the books of the Bible), can be
empirically verified and rationally studied by using basic rules of evidence and laws of logic. There is sufficient evidence that the historical
biblical documents making up the holy Bible are internally consistent
and factually true. The Bible clearly states that all human beings are sinful (Gen. 8:21; Psalm 14:1-3; John 3:19; Rom. 3:9-18, 23), but that
Jesus Christ died for their sins and rose from the dead (Mark 10:45;
16:6; Luke 24:45-48; 1 Cor. 15:1-8). Human beings can receive forgiveness from God for their sins by believing in this gospel of Jesus
Christ, believing in the work Jesus has done for their souls (John 8:12;
11:25-26; Acts 2:38; 26:15; Eph. 1:17; 1 John 2:12).

Viewed in the light of all this, The Lord of the Rings books and
movies have a strongly moral Christian worldview with Christian
metaphors and allegories, whereas the Harry Potter books and movies
have a strongly pagan, occult, and gnostic worldview that borrows
redemptive elements from Christianity. How can this be—that Harry
Potter can embody an anti-Christian worldview while at the same time
using redemptive elements from Christianity to tell its stories?

Well, sinful people of conscious or unconscious ominous intent can distort the gospel story for their own agendas. Thus a movie or work of art can mix together an evil, abhorrent worldview with positive redemptive elements. Or, as detective novelist Raymond Chandler noted in his famous essay "The Simple Art of Murder," "In everything that can be called art there is a quality of redemption. It may be pure tragedy, if it is high tragedy, and it may be pity and irony, and it may be the raucous laughter of the strong man."[8]

## DETERMINING WORLDVIEW

In today's entertainment industry, many movies like to be all things to all people so that they can attract the widest audience possible. Thus some movies might have a positive Christian or moral worldview but also contain some vulgar content appealing to the fourteen-year-old boy, who remains the primary target audience of many Hollywood movies. This attempt to appeal to a wide audience without alienating the teenage boy can make it hard to identify the movie's dominant worldview.

Also many people working in the entertainment industry think that movies should not be didactic; hence, they must be subtle. Filmmakers often mistake ambiguity for subtlety however. Some of these same filmmakers believe that their role is not to answer the questions raised by the premise of the story, but to let the audience determine the answers for themselves. This belief also can lead to an ambiguous premise and an ambiguous worldview.

Chapter IX, "Asking the Right Questions About Frodo and Harry," will help you to determine the dominant worldview in a work of narrative art or a movie. For now, however, we'd like to compare movies to a car trip. A movie's worldview is like the overall design of a car. The premise is where you are going. The plot is how you get there and the obstacles you face along the way. The characters are the passengers. The premise can also be seen as the main proposition that drives the narrative or story, like the engine that drives the car. To help you determine the dominant worldview of the movie, you should look at the premise. As you do so, the end resolution of the conflict between the protagonist or hero and the antagonist or villain can be one of the most important expressions of the movie's dominant worldview.

Finally, the worldview is often related to the environment, world, or atmosphere in which the story takes place. For example, The Lord of the Rings and Harry Potter both take place in fantasy worlds; however, in the former God's laws remain intact, while in the latter God's laws are suspended or absent.

The Lord of the Rings is an epic story that takes place in a mythic fantasy realm where supernatural forces are in conflict, but the Harry Potter books and movies take place at a school for witchcraft and wizardry. The witches and sorcerers at the school, including the students, come into conflict with the outside world of the nonmagic folk, or Muggles, who sometimes even try to kill the witches and sorcerers. The design of both sagas and the world or environment in which they take place are different, even though they share other qualities that seem, at least on the surface, to be the same.

## DIFFERENT KINDS OF STORIES

Different kinds of stories meet different needs. For example, a work of fiction evokes a different response from us than a work of nonfiction. Likewise a mystery story about a private detective searching for clues in a complex murder case satisfies different needs in people than a science fiction story about technologically superior alien invaders from Mars.

In a categorization of dramatic stories, Aristotle said that there were only four basic plots: man against man; man against nature; man against himself; and man against the supernatural or sub-natural, including aliens.

Aristotle's categories help us to evaluate the premise or main proposition in a story, but they may not help us determine whether the story fits the Christian worldview. Another traditional literary approach may be more helpful. It divides stories into five different styles:

1. Mythic, in a traditional sense (we use the word myth in an entirely different sense later): The hero or protagonist(s) triumphs by an act of God or gods.

2. Heroic: The triumph of the hero or protagonist(s) by his own means.

3. High Ironic: The triumph of the hero or protagonist(s) by a quirk of fate.

4. Low Ironic: The failure of the hero or protagonist(s) by a quirk of fate.

5. Demonic: The defeat of the hero or protagonist(s) by evil, demons, etc.

A story that fits the Christian version of the traditional mythic story, where the God of the Bible or Jesus Christ helps the hero or protagonist overcome his or her antagonist, is a story that fits the Christian worldview. A story, however, where the hero or protagonist, especially a Christian one, is defeated by demons is probably not a story that Christians should want to see, because it contradicts their worldview and the worldview of the Bible.

Literary and film scholars have used another word to help them discuss different kinds of stories: *genre*. As Steve Neale points out in *Genre and Hollywood* (Routledge, 2000), recent scholars have noted that the ways in which literary scholars discuss these different kinds of stories has often differed from the ways in which film scholars do. In fact, the very use of the term *genre* has come into question. It even confuses Mr. Neale, who lumps together the categories of nonfiction, fiction, and poetry with the categories of mystery, science fiction, western, etc.

To eliminate some, if not all, of the confusion in this area of study, it may be best to use the terminology taught at the Radio-TV-Film Department at Northwestern University in the late 1970s and early 1980s. At that time students there learned to separate "modes" of communication from genre.

This separation may not answer all questions. After all, whenever you make a distinction between two categories, there is a possibility that at some point the categories will overlap. This separation between mode and genre does help us, however, to distinguish between such broad categories as nonfiction and poetry and such smaller categories as mystery and science fiction.

A mode of communication is a general form or manner of expression, such as fiction, nonfiction, poetry, prose, documentary nonfiction film, narrative fiction film, animation, and experimental or avant-garde film. Sometimes modes can be combined, as in narrative fiction films using documentary techniques such as cinema verité.

A genre is a specific body, group, cycle, or category of works that resemble one another because they share a sufficient number of similar motifs, themes, styles, imagery, visual designs, ideas, character types, story formulas, and plot devices. Examples of different genres are fantasy, historical epic, biography, musical, science fiction, detective, crime story, mystery, horror, and comedy. By looking at the common traits that connect similar works, readers, viewers, and listeners can better understand each genre and each work that seems to be part of a particular genre. Genres can be combined, as in science fiction/horror novels and movies such as *Frankenstein* or *Alien*, or musical comedies such as *Singin' in the Rain*, although most pundits usually refer to the predominant genre. Genre categories are useful because they take the broader categories of modes and break them down into particular patterns for closer study.

Both The Lord of the Rings books and movies and the Harry Potter books and movies are in the narrative fiction mode. They also belong to the genre category known as fantasy, even though Lord of the Rings also belongs to the genre categories of epic adventure and Arthurian romance.

The word *fantasy* has a problematic definition that seems overbroad. Stated simply, fantasy is a work that takes place in an implausible, unreal world filled with implausible, bizarre, grotesque, and/or extremely imaginary creatures and situations. That does not mean, of course, that within the imaginary world in which the fantasy occurs there are no realistic characters, settings, and situations. Thus Lord of the Rings includes descriptions and images of horses very similar to the horses we know in real life. Also Harry Potter books and movies contain discussions and images of books that are much like the books we know in real life, except that the books sometimes have fantastic, implausible, "magical" powers.

Most modes of communication and most genres elicit no value judgments regardless of one's worldview. People of practically any worldview can enjoy reading or watching books, movies, videos, and television programs that belong to any number of modes and genres without feeling guilty because the mode or genre violates an important philosophical, theological, moral, or political doctrine. This is not true for committed Christians in the case of genres and modes such as the mad slasher horror movie or works of explicit pornography.

Some Christians have wrongly rejected the fantasy genre because its works contain implausible worlds with implausible creatures and situations that can't be true except in one's imagination. It is the worldview, however—including the philosophy, theology, and morality within the work—that makes the work false, heretical, or evil. Furthermore, there are varying degrees of falsehood, heresy, and evil, and, as we said earlier, many works can also combine elements from different worldviews. Even the first two Harry Potter books and movies include a brief mention of Christmas, although neither of these occult books or movies contains any explicit positive references to Jesus Christ or his birth. Of course, The Lord of the Rings books and movies don't contain any explicit positive references to Christianity either, but there are many implied positive references to the Christian worldview of the original author, J. R. R. Tolkien, in both the books and the movies, including symbolic references to the Holy Spirit. Furthermore, as we discuss elsewhere, The Lord of the Rings stories contain philosophical and moral beliefs and attitudes that fit a Christian worldview, whereas the Harry Potter stories contain elements that violate basic Christian beliefs and principles.

## CLOSE ENCOUNTERS WITH THE DIVINE BEING

Many stories focus on a heroic figure who overcomes trials and tribulations to defeat some kind of evil or to attain a valuable, positive goal. Film genre scholar Thomas Sobchack talks about medieval romance stories in this way:

> A protagonist either has or develops great and special skills and overcomes insurmountable obstacles in extraordinary situations to successfully achieve some desired goal, usually the restitution of order to the world invoked by the narrative. The protagonists confront the human, natural, or supernatural powers that have improperly assumed control over the world and eventually defeat them.[9]

This hero myth does not just occur in adventure movies and medieval romance, however. In fact, some scholars, such as New Ager Joseph Campbell, believe that the hero myth occurs in nearly every story ever created. For example, there can be stories or myths about people where the hero or protagonist fails or is defeated. Thus the hero may leave his home on a quest where he encounters new environments, new characters, and new situations that test his courage, stamina, and strength, but he fails these tests, or the antagonists in the stories actually defeat him. Also, in many modern dramas, the protagonist is a lost soul who goes on a psychological journey, an inner struggle, that results either in triumph, failure, defeat, or some combination thereof.

Some people are under the mistaken impression that to call something a hero myth means that the story is completely false or untrue. Nothing could be further from the truth. In fact, the personal lives of many historical figures can be compared to the basic structure of the hero myth. For example, Abraham Lincoln is a mythic hero to many people. As a young man, he left his rural background to pursue his political career and became president of the United States. While he was in office, the heartbreaking Civil War tested his courage, stamina, and strength. His story provides many lessons for those of us in real life, just as the fictional story of Frodo and Sam in The Lord of the Rings has provided many lessons for different people of various walks of life and worldviews.

To call a story mythic is not to call it a total lie. A myth is any real or fictional story, recurring theme, or character type that appeals to the consciousness of a people by embodying major cultural ideals and/or by giving expression to deep, commonly felt, and/or transcendent emotions and/or rational or irrational ideas. The story of the hero is one such myth, and it can occur in either fiction or nonfiction. Sometimes it even occurs in science fact, such as the story of Galileo, whose ideas were challenged and for a time defeated by the leaders in the scientific community of his day.

Of course, as our opening discussion implied, the greatest hero myth or hero story is the story of Jesus Christ, who died for our sins but rose from the dead by an act of God and who offers us a deep personal relationship with God. This relationship, empowered by communion and fellowship with the Holy Spirit, leads us into all truth and eventually will lead us into eternal life with the one true God, the Father, Son, and Holy Spirit.

Thus the greatest story of them all, the tale of the Christ and his church, is the greatest, truest myth because in it God offers us a majestic, profound, personal, sacred encounter with the transcendent, holy, infinite, almighty, and deeply mysterious but infinitely loving Divine Being who created us. Tolkien recognized this in his work, not only The Lord of the Rings but also in his other writings, such as *The Silmarillion*, the mythic back-story to The Lord of the Rings. All true art may indeed have a redemptive quality, but the most redemptive works of art are those that skillfully allude, either implicitly or explicitly, to the greatest story ever told.

## CONCLUSION

Christianity is superior to all other worldviews because it is logical, it explains many different kinds of phenomenon, and it fits the facts. As such, it provides a rational justification for judging what is good or evil, right or wrong, true or false, and proper or improper. It also gives human beings a meaningful love and provides us with a set of documents, the Bible, that can be empirically and rationally verified. By looking at the worldview in a work of literature, cinema, video, or television, we can determine if that work reaches the highest levels of truth, justice, goodness, love, and beauty embodied by Jesus Christ and the one true God, as depicted in the Bible, the Word of God, and in the traditions God has inspired.

As we analyze the differences among stories, we can examine the motifs, meanings, values, and principles that each story evokes. Their common patterns can give us insights into truth, reality, human nature, God, and the spirit of the imagination. Finally, by studying stories about heroes, including the heroes that populate B movies and the heroes that populate great literature, including the Bible and The Lord of the Rings, we may eventually gain a powerful, life-changing sense of the nature of the greatest hero who ever lived—Jesus Christ. This is true just as much for the children and teenagers in your family as it is for the adults.

# VIII

# THE CHURCH, THE MEDIA, AND THE CULTURE

*Over the past 20 years we have seen the nation's theological views slowly become less aligned with the Bible. Americans still revere the Bible and like to think of themselves as Bible-believing people, but the evidence suggests otherwise. Christians have increasingly been adopting spiritual views that come from Islam, Wicca, secular humanism, the eastern religions and other sources. Because we remain a largely Bible-illiterate society, few are alarmed or even aware of the slide toward syncretism—a belief system that blindly combines beliefs from many different faith perspectives.*[1]

GEORGE BARNA

In the past the church shaped Western civilization, otherwise known as Christendom, with an aim to heal the sick, feed the hungry, clothe the poor, and create art to worship a just and loving Creator who gave form and function to reality. Now our culture is shaped by the mass media of entertainment. The results are confusion at best and the most vile paganism at worst.

The Barna survey quoted above also shows that a shockingly large number of Americans believes that when Jesus Christ was on earth, he committed sins, which would mean that his death on the cross could not have been a sinless offering. Sad to say, most of those who contend that Jesus sinned are under thirty-eight years of age, the very generation impacted by the Supreme Court's crazed decision to remove prayer and faith from the public classroom.

If Jesus is no longer a sufficient sacrifice for our sins, then it is no wonder that almost half the population believes that deliverance from eternal condemnation for one's sins is earned rather than received as a free gift from God through Jesus' death and resurrection. Thus half of all adults argue that anyone who "is generally good or does enough good things for others during their life will earn a place in Heaven."[2] Of course, this is highly illogical because anyone who is not suffering from short-term memory loss understands through common human relationships the biblical truth that no person is righteous. Nearly 75 percent of all adults believe that people have the potential to be good, which means that these people don't need salvation.

Therefore, it is not surprising, though it is heartbreaking, that 40 percent of all adults, especially younger adults, hold the confused belief that "the Bible, the Koran and the Book of Mormon are all different expressions of the same spiritual truths."[3] Of course, if they bother to read these books, they would find that each claims a unique way of salvation that excludes all other ways. A large majority of both adults and teenagers contends that there is no absolute moral truth and that truth is always relative to the individual and the circumstances. Many argue that nothing is wrong per se, including abortion, suicide, or euthanasia. The common rubric seems to be: "It's just a matter of opinion."

## NICE IS NOT GOOD ENOUGH

Moral relativism may be the reason the antihero in movies has become so prominent that people are now actually considering the antihero as somehow "good." For instance, the protagonists in *Ocean's 11*—starring George Clooney, Brad Pitt, and the rest of the new rat pack—are nice, but clearly they are not good. They lie, they cheat, and, of course, they steal. They are the heroes, and we are apparently supposed to root for them.

Harry Potter is another example of a hero who is nice but who is not good. He uses deception and disobeys rules, and instead of being rebuked, he is often rewarded. Frodo, the hero of Lord of the Rings, makes mistakes, but ultimately he tries to do the right thing.

This theology of relativism is also creeping into the church. In the United States, we are experiencing an unprecedented 22 percent decline of commitment to Christ among children and teenagers (a personal observation by George Barna). Thom Rainer has noted that fifty years ago 70 percent of the children had heard the gospel and were familiar with the Bible. Today that number is just 4 percent.[4] As in other countries where the church has collapsed, many in the believing evangelical church are grasping at straws and forming alliances with strange non-Christian bedfellows to try to slow the fall.

These nonbelievers are nice people who often preach a legalistic theology of works and even seem conservative. When the producer of a radio program hosted by one of these pleasant non-Christian people, who was being promoted within the church, told me not to talk about Jesus Christ, I (Ted) said that Jesus was the reason for all that I do. Soon afterward this non-Christian host was lauded at a largely evangelical event as if his message of legalism and moralism would solve our nation's ills. This wonderful host has repeatedly rejected the claims of Jesus Christ, which he says he has clearly heard and understands. If he has heard the gospel and rejected it repeatedly, the church should clearly recognize that he is not a Christian.

In a way these conservative non-Christian leaders are unconsciously guarding the Adversary's right flank, just as the anti-Christian liberal leaders were guarding the left flank in the era of the social gospel. Neither lawlessness nor legalism will cure our culture's ills.

As Paul writes in Ephesians 4:1-32, God does not want us to live as the godless pagans do, in the futility and darkness of their thinking. Instead, we must live a worthy life and gently, humbly, patiently, lovingly make every effort to keep the unity of the Holy Spirit through peace. There is to be only one faith, one Lord and one God, who has given each person his measure of divine grace as Jesus the Christ has apportioned it. Jesus prepares God's people for works of service "for building up the body of Christ, until we all attain to the unity of the faith and of the knowledge of the Son of God, to mature manhood, to the measure of the stature of the fullness of Christ, so that we may no longer be children, tossed to and fro by the waves and carried about by every wind of doctrine, by human cunning, by craftiness in deceitful schemes. Rather, speaking the truth in love, we are to grow up in every way into him who is the head, into Christ, from whom the whole body, joined and held together by every joint with which it is equipped, when each part is working properly, makes the body grow so that it builds itself up in love" (Eph. 4:12-16).

This picture of a healthy, growing church cannot be realized if we listen to people, no matter how well intentioned and smart, who do not know Jesus Christ or who practice a theology of relativism. "Therefore," Paul writes in Ephesians 4:25 and 5:1-2, "having put away falsehood, let each one of you speak the truth with his neighbor. . . . Be imitators of God, as beloved children. And walk in love, as Christ loved us and gave himself up for us, a fragrant offering and sacrifice to God." Furthermore, Paul instructs, "Let no one deceive you with empty words, for because of these things the wrath of God comes upon the sons of disobedience. Therefore do not associate with them; for at one time you were darkness, but now you are light in the Lord. Walk as children of light (for the fruit of light is found in all that is good and right and true), and try to discern what is pleasing to the Lord" (Eph. 5:6-10).

## BEYOND THE CREEDS

While there are creedal and moral absolutes, there are also areas of interpretation that are not creedal and where different communities of believers have taken different positions. The church historically has always had five different perspectives toward culture. Each of these perspectives can be supported with the appropriate Bible verses, but none of them can be shown to be the "correct" reading to the exclusion of the others. So none of them is creedal or a measure of orthodoxy.

Yale theologian H. Richard Niebuhr first distinguished between the five approaches Christians have historically taken with regard to their world in his book *Christ and Culture*.[5] His distinctions have been modified and clarified for the purposes of this book.

The first position could be called "retreat from culture," though Niebuhr calls it "Christ Against Culture." He cites the Mennonite and

Amish communities as the obvious examples of this tradition, though he could have also referred to the monastic tradition in the Roman Catholic church. While there are rich traditions of service within these groups, the world is viewed as a place from which to escape into communities of "separated brethren." The Schleitheim Confession of the Anabaptists (1527) argued, "Since all who do not walk in the obedience of faith are a great abomination before God, it is not possible for anything to grow or issue from them except abominable things. God further admonishes us to withdraw from Babylon and the earthly Egypt that we may not be partakers of the pain and suffering which the Lord will bring upon them."

The second perspective, which Niebuhr calls "The Christ of Culture," tends to equate creation and redemption and can be seen in those groups that identify Christ with utopian socialism as well as those who identify Christ with American culture. Those who follow this tradition hail Jesus as the Messiah of their society, the fulfiller of its hopes and aspirations, the perfecter of its true faith, the source of its holiest spirit. For these people there is hardly any difference between Christ and the culture. These adherents view Christ as the moral example who points us to a perfect society.

The third approach, which Niebuhr calls "Christ Above Culture," is occupied by the centrists who live within the world though they are not of the world. These centrists refuse either to take the position of the anti-cultural radicals or to join with those who accommodate Christ to the culture.

The fourth tradition is "Christ and Culture in Paradox," which refuses either to reject culture or to confuse culture with Christianity. They see these as two different realms, not two antagonistic realms. In creation God gives us work, service, pleasure, government, and family. In redemption he gives us the church, the Word, and the sacraments. The Christian who follows the "Christ and Culture in Paradox" tradition participates in culture but not as a means of grace. Living in the culture is rather an aspect of being human, not merely of being a Christian.

The final category is "Christ, the Transformer of Culture," which emphasizes God's lordship over all of creation and all aspects of life. Niebuhr appeals to John's Gospel as an example of this approach. Here Christ is "the Word made flesh"—not only the priest of redemption but also the king of creation. This tradition, which is represented by Augustine and Calvin, takes the world seriously and contends that Christians have the potential not only to exercise leadership in the culture but to present the gospel as well. God loves the world, not just individuals in it (Rom. 8:20-23).

Those of the "Christ Transforming Culture" tradition would view culture as a distinct, though related, part of Christ's universal reign. While creating a movie, building a house, or raising a family may not be the redemptive activities of the kingdom of God, they are important activities to which Christians realize a call, because they are commanded by the universal Lord in the "cultural mandate" of the early chapters of Genesis. Though human activity can never bring salvation, the activity of Christian men and women does bring a certain transforming, redemptive element as they live out their callings in distinction and honor, serving both to attract non-Christians to the gospel and to bring civil righteousness, justice, and compassion to bear on human relationships.

The church has historically moved through a cycle from one point of view to the other. During the middle of the twentieth century, the church retreated from culture. Then the church took up the battle cry of cultural warfare to resist the moral decay in our society. Now the church is beginning to move out as ambassadors for Jesus Christ to redeem the culture.

Whatever cultural position you, your local church, or your denomination adopt, we are called to develop the discernment to know right from wrong, the wisdom to choose the right, the knowledge to pursue the right, and the understanding to persevere. "For God gave us a spirit not of fear but of power and love and self-control" (2 Tim. 1:7).

## "TO" OR "FROM"—THAT IS THE QUESTION

Joseph E. Coleson, Professor of Old Testament at Nazarene Theological Seminary, Kansas City, Missouri, pinpointed the primary reason the church has divided into five perspectives toward culture in an article written for *Movieguide*®. He notes the misinterpretation of the meaning of *holy* and *holiness*:

> In our secularized Western culture, Christians often think of holiness as something from the sainted few. Non-Christians, if they think of

holiness at all, may find it a concept for ridicule or even for censure. Not too many of us think of holiness as something to be desired and sought after, but the truth is everyone is, or is becoming, holy to something or someone.

So what is holiness, really? What does the word mean, and what does the Bible mean when, for example, God says, "Be holy, for I am holy" (Leviticus 11:44, and other passages)? Do we shy away from holiness because we don't understand it?

If we want to know what it means to be holy, we must look at the concept of holiness in two steps. If Christians, especially, omit the first step, we will fall down on the second, and produce a mock holiness that only repels, never attracts.

## TO BE HOLY IS TO BE SEPARATE

Our first step is to notice that "holy/holiness" was a common word in the ancient world of the Hebrew Bible; it occurs in all the languages related to Hebrew. In Hebrew, its basic form is *qadosh* (ka-DOHSH). *Qadosh* means, first and foremost, "to be separate." In the Hebrew Bible (the Old Testament) and in documents from all of Israel's ancient neighbors, many things were spoken of as "holy," "separate," "special."

In the Hebrew Bible, God often spoke of himself as holy. When describing God, holy means transcendent—distinct from the universe of space and time that we inhabit. God is separate from the universe because God existed before the universe, God made the universe, and God does not depend on the universe or anything in it for God's continued existence. Rather, the universe and all it contains depend on God. When the Old Testament says God is "holy," it means God is transcendent.

Then, what does it mean for a human to be holy? It means for us, also, to be separate, but of course we are not transcendent. How, then, are we separate? . . .

Humans, too, were/are set apart, dedicated, made holy to God alone. Within ancient Israel, the priests and Levites were holy—set apart for—the service of God in God's Tabernacle (later, the Temple of Solomon in Jerusalem). Israel as a nation was a holy people, because God chose Israel, first of all the peoples, to be separate to Him.

But, Israel did not always follow Yahweh's call to be holy to him alone. (Yahweh—pronounced YAH-way—is the Old Testament Hebrew name for God.) Often, Israel chose to mix the worship of Yahweh with worship of other gods, most notably Baal of the

Canaanites. When that happened, Israel no longer was separated—set apart, holy—to Yahweh alone.

## SEPARATE "FROM," OR SEPARATE "TO"?

Why did Israel have so much difficulty, and why do modern Christians often have great difficulty, in being holy to God, totally set apart to God? That question brings us to our second step in considering what "holy" really means. The answer, and the second step, is as simple as whether we choose a two-letter or a four-letter preposition to follow the word "holy." Are we holy "from," or are we holy "to"?

Too often, the ancient Israelite and modern Christian alike have chosen to be "holy from" certain things, assuming that shows they were/are holy to God. So the ancient Israelites did not eat pork, for example, and some assumed that meant they were holy to Yahweh, even if they prayed to Baal as well as to Yahweh to bring the rain to water their wheat fields and fill their cisterns.

Too often today, conservative Christians think that if they don't (pick one or more): drink alcohol; smoke or chew tobacco; play the horses or the casinos; dance; rob a bank—their list of "don'ts" proves they are holy to God. But, all this can prove is they are moral and decent people.

In fact, separation "from" things, in its worst form, is legalism and hypocrisy, and has been responsible for more children, raised in Christian families, rebelling and leaving the faith, than any other single cause. Some of us were/are "holy from" movies in the cinemas, but will watch anything on our cable channel or on video. Some of us can become so focused on being "holy from" the things we outlaw that we become snobs, even become vicious and hateful toward neighbors, fellow church members, or even family members, who do not share our convictions on our hot-button issues.

Holiness defined as separation from a set of external behaviors or possessions is, at best, healthy self-discipline. At its worst, it is self-delusional, relationship-destroying, deadening, and deadly legalism and hypocrisy.

But, separation "to"! Now, that's another matter! . . .True holiness is separation to God. It is entering into and progressing in a relationship with God that makes God increasingly one's Best Friend. It is separation "from" things only because they harm or hinder one's relationship with God and God's people, and hinder one's ability to demonstrate to others the awesomeness of the God who loved us enough to die for us.

. . . Christians are not holy because we are moral, ethical people. We are moral, ethical people because the God we love is the God of justice, righteousness, lovingkindness, mercy, grace and truth. God's people take on God's moral, ethical character.

Don't be satisfied with being separate "from" a few things, and calling it religion, or even holiness. In every area of your life—family, work, church, finances, recreation, entertainment, everything!!—start being truly, deeply, thoroughly, passionately holy to the God who loves you![6]

## CAN ENTERTAINMENT BE HOLY?

The church has had a love-hate relationship with art, music, and drama for centuries. Although modern drama as we know it was invented by the church in the Middle Ages to help the illiterate populace understand the gospel, the Mystery or Miracle Plays, as these Christian dramas were known, quickly became suspect. The clergy felt that the dramas were overshadowing their sermons. Therefore, Pope Innocent III outlawed drama. The dramatists, whose creative abilities and desires were a gift from God, went into the alleys and the beer halls to exercise their God-given gifts in not-so-God-ordained ways.

A similar scenario has happened many times throughout history. Roman Catholic theologian and scholar Michael Jones blames the growth of Protestantism on the willingness of the Protestants to use the newfangled printing press to print Bibles while the Catholic church rejected the new technology of communication. Centuries later, at the beginning of the use of film, a cardinal in Paris was shocked by movies being shown in the Cathedral of Notre Dame (movies on the life and passion of Jesus Christ, by the way) and banned film from the church, thus turning the new medium over to the very people most opposed to the church. Edison tried to give the rights to the motion picture technology to his denomination, but they rejected it. The first radio broadcast station was located in a church in Pittsburgh, but the rector of the church demanded that the younger associate get rid of it.

## PROCLAIMING IN THE MARKETPLACE

Five Greek words are translated by the English word *preaching* in the New Testament. Sixty-three percent of the time, Jesus uses the Greek word *keryssa*, related to *kerygma*, which means to proclaim or herald in the marketplace. The word *keryssa* was relevant to the people Jesus was talking to because they were familiar with the Roman heralds who ran into the marketplace every morning and shouted out the news of the emperor to the buyers and sellers.

Thus Jesus Christ has always commanded his people to go into the marketplace of ideas to herald the Good News. When Christians do so, as in the Protestant Reformation and the evangelization of South Korea, the church grows and prospers. When Christians fail to go into the marketplace, the church shrinks in size and suffers.

## THE CHRISTIAN VIEW OF ART AND COMMUNICATIONS

Several years ago I (Ted) co-chaired an Art and Communications Committee of several prominent theologians for the Coalition on Revival to set forth *The Christian World View of Art and Communication*.[7] We believed that Christians need to have influence in the mass media of entertainment. Our dialogue produced a concrete vision of what was foundationally required to do that. The following are basic principles upon which a relationship between the arts and a Christian worldview are based:

> "In the beginning God created" and "In the beginning was the Word." God is the Author of creation and communication. As the supreme Creator and Communicator, He is the Source of art and communication.
>
> God has given all authority in heaven and on earth to His Son, Jesus Christ. Since Jesus Christ is entitled to have lordship over all areas of life, Christians must bring all art and communication under His authority.
>
> Art and communication are part of God's created order. They cannot be labeled Christian or un-Christian. However, they can be used for good or evil.
>
> Art and communication are neither synonymous nor mutually exclusive functions in God's economy. Communication is the act of sharing thoughts, ideas, information, and needs. The arts, whether or not they communicate, are expressions of God's creativity manifested through man.
>
> Man, created in the image of God, has the capacity to create and

communicate. Therefore, all artistic endeavor and communications involve more than technical skills. Their intended purpose is to glorify God. To accomplish this, all art and communication must be brought into captivity to the mind of Christ.

Christ is the standard of excellence. "Whatever you do, work heartily, as for the Lord and not for men. . . ." (Col. 3:23). Within the framework of that excellence, art and communication should reflect the highest quality of creative work possible, given the resources available. Since all abilities are God-given, we can achieve excellence when we submit them to the lordship of Jesus Christ and the guidance of God. This guidance comes from communication with God through prayer, study of His written Word, and other Biblical disciplines vital to being a Christian.

Art and communication have a great influence on society in shaping man's view of reality. A career in these fields should be considered a worthy vocation. To achieve such a career, Christians should discern and develop their God-given talents.

It is legitimate for Christians to engage in art and communication without the need to include overt Christian symbolism or content. A Christian may participate in any area of art and communication as long as he submits himself to the lordship of Jesus Christ in accordance with His written Word, and acts in the conviction of faith, for "without faith it is impossible to please [God]" (Heb. 11:6).

## THEOLOGY OF ART

Up until the twentieth century, there was an active theology of art and beauty placing God the Holy Spirit as the guiding influence in the arts and communication media. However, in reaction to modern secularism the church retreated from culture. The church is emerging from this retreat, but in the process has regrettably lost many of its common symbols and modes of art and communication. Therefore, to a large degree, sacramental and incarnational modes of communication and art are often misunderstood by the contemporary church. This church often simply proclaims the milk of the gospel, as noted in Hebrews 5, and stops before getting to the meat of Hebrews 6. Some Christian colleges and schools have created either/or theories of art and communication and have neglected to note the both/and of the gospel about Jesus Christ, who was both God and man. These theories diminish the biblical view of art and communications.

Traditionally, there are four philosophies of art. Plato said that art represented the ideal. Aristotle reacted to Plato and considered art in a materialistic context as something made by man and contrary to nature. The Roman Horace tried to blend the ideas of the two Greek philosophers and defined art as something that delights and informs. The Bible emphasizes that art should concern the true, the good, and the beautiful.

As a result of the materialism of the modern culture, the last fifty years have primarily followed Aristotle's definition. Art has been too often defined as anything contrary to nature or pushing the envelope. In this view, if one movie features female nudity from the waist up, the next has to feature full frontal female nudity, and the next has to have frontal male nudity, etc.

## HOLLYWOOD'S "THEOLOGY" OF ART

In the last half century, a new aristocracy has emerged in the United States. The entertainer, whether an athlete, movie star, or news announcer, has become the new upper class. Not only do these Hollywood idols and their compatriots make incredible salaries (Michael Eisner earned over $350 million in stock options one year; several Hollywood and sports stars earned over $20 million; and the major television news anchors earned over $5 million), but they also wield incredible power in every area of life by shaping the thoughts, dreams, and concerns of our culture. As actress Susan Sarandon has so aptly pointed out, movie stars are dangerous because "we are the keeper of the dreams."

The reason we have this new aristocracy is that we have become wealthy beyond our wildest expectations as a result of our freedoms and opportunities. In the process we have turned away from the true joy of residing in God's grace. Instead we seek amusement in the world, the flesh, and the devil. In light of our precipitous backsliding, a few entertainment moguls have seized the opportunity of our addiction to pleasure to bamboozle us into misinterpreting the First Amendment to read that everything from pedophilia to pornography is "protected speech"— except, of course, Christian speech. The reason these people spend millions of dollars to stretch the notion of "protected speech" beyond any reasonable intent of the Constitution's framers is to protect their profitable sale of salacious pornography and extreme violence to vulnerable adolescents, children, and adults.

This new media aristocracy has developed its own form of noblesse oblige by selling us on the idea that the government should cover the cost of all social programs. They have reinterpreted sin to mean politically incorrect speech and have carefully removed any onus from the family-destroying sins of adultery and sodomy. As linguist and political analyst Noam Chomsky has said, "The United States is unusual among the industrial democracies in the rigidity of the system of ideological control—'indoctrination,' we might say—exercised through the mass media."[8]

The importance of this new elite demands the attention of the church. Please pray for the people who hold responsible positions of extreme national and international importance within the mass media of entertainment. Please pray that the church can help them make only redemptive, virtuous works that honor Christ.

## IS INTOLERANCE EVER OKAY?

Several years ago I (Ted) participated in a discussion with the major networks and movie studios regarding advocacy groups. We were the only registered Christian advocacy group, but there were other groups representing homosexuals, Jews, African-Americans, and Arab-Americans, as well as many other racial and religious affinity groups. The senior executives from Hollywood went out of their way to be tolerant, clearly scared that they would offend somebody.

It is understandable why the mass media places a premium on tolerance, given the increasingly diverse culture in which we live. Of course, some of this tolerance is aimed at diluting the influence of Christians in our culture, but most is born out of trying to reach the entire demographic range in the United States.

However, in stark contrast to the media's obeisance to tolerance, several years before this UCLA-organized event, the late intellectual and humorist Steve Allen spoke on this important topic at the National Religious Broadcasters at my invitation. Allen claimed to be an atheist who read the Bible every day, but since his wife was a committed Christian, he decided to tackle this difficult subject.

Steve waxed eloquent and explained why intolerance was sometimes the only option. He asked the audience to put themselves in Moses' place: If you were a Jew and came upon a burning bush where it was clear that

God himself was speaking to you, and the event was so frightening that you fell on your face before him, and God told you he is a jealous God who would have no other Gods before him and told you exactly what judgment you faced if you refused to obey him, what would you do? Steve concluded that you would obey the awesome almighty, creator God whom you had just met in person, and you would forever after be intolerant of other gods. In other words, the divine distinctives of Judaism, as well as Christianity and Islam, often compel intolerance if you believe that your faith comes directly from the Almighty.

Yes, intolerance to relativism is appropriate. It is not "just a matter of opinion." There is an absolute truth that sets us free.

## CORROSION OF THE CHRISTIAN WORLDVIEW

Recently I (Ted) was on a national so-called conservative talk show whose host defended the Harry Potter books by attacking the straw men of his imagination who stood against his point of view. He believed that Harry Potter was harmless and that anyone with a contrary point of view was wrong.

Our position is neither black nor white but reflects the world that God reveals in his Scriptures. For many people, Harry Potter is harmless. A few people will be sucked into the world of witchcraft. Most witchcraft is phony, and God tells us that most of these people are charlatans and foolish, but even the charlatans lead people astray and get them to worship idols and accept false doctrines. Our goal is to help people on both sides (those who say that they are not affected and those who are affected) to deal with the moral, psychological, and spiritual aspects that corrode the Christian worldview.

Quite simply, God abhors witchcraft, and so should we. God's command in the Hebrew Bible/Old Testament is to avoid exposure to witchcraft, wizardry, sorcery, and any of the magical arts. This passage reads very clearly: "Let no one be found among you who sacrifices his son or daughter in the fire, who practices divination or sorcery, interprets omens, engages in witchcraft, or casts spells, or who is a medium or spiritist or who consults the dead" (Deut. 18:10 -11 NIV).

Because this command is in the Old Testament, a few Christians have said that it does not apply today to Christians. Not only does this reasoning not hold water hermeneutically, but also the commands against witchcraft are mentioned throughout the New Testament. In Acts 8 the apostle Peter condemns Simon the sorcerer to hell. The book of Revelation states several times that sorcerers will not enter into heaven.

*For without are dogs, and sorcerers, and whoremongers, and murderers, and idolaters, and whosoever loveth and maketh a lie. (Rev. 22:15 KJV)*

*But as for the cowardly, the faithless, the detestable, as for murderers, the sexually immoral, sorcerers, idolaters, and all liars, their portion will be in the lake that burns with fire and sulfur, which is the second death. (Rev. 21:8)*

God's injunction against witchcraft, sorcery, and the like applies as much today to Christians as it always has to observant Jews.

Ideas have consequences. You can't do the deed unless you have a creed. Making distinctions is very important when it comes to having a proper moral theology. God wants us to worship him with our whole mind, not just our emotion. Thus logical, intelligent thought and an intelligent, logical art and science of biblical interpretation are absolutely essential if we are to worship Jesus Christ in truth and light, and love our neighbors as ourselves.

## DID GOD REALLY SAY?

Regrettably, an anti-Christian relativism, which says that there are no absolute truths and no moral absolutes, has invaded many Christian ministries. For example, one writer for a Christian ministry, when talking about contradictory Christian views on a particular movie, came up with this conclusion: "This [the very fact of contradictory views] just proves that movie messages, like beauty, are in the eye of the beholder." The writer just assumed that relativism was the best conclusion, instead of asking himself whether some of the views expressed by the Christian writers were right and some were wrong. He also failed to consider whether the movie might have had an ambivalent worldview that caused some of its apparently contradictory messages. Nor did it occur to the writer that the movie may have contained more than one message at the same time and that some or most of the Christian critics just chose to deal with one or two of the messages rather than explore all of the movie's layers of meaning.

Imagine telling the Holocaust survivors who suffered from the impact of Dr. Joseph Goebbels's feature film *I Accuse* that film messages are only in the eye of the beholder. This film convinced the German people to support so-called "mercy killing" instead of opposing it. "Mercy killing" was the Nazi code word for the Holocaust. *I Accuse* is a very subtle film, but the message was not in the eye of the beholder.

Or imagine telling the millions of people who came to Christ through *The Jesus Film* that their conversion and newfound personal relationship with Jesus Christ resulted from just their interpretation of the movie—not from the truth. This "eye of the beholder" statement, like the rest of relativism, turns communications inside out.

Christians believe that we can know what God said and what God meant, even when he said, "Don't eat of this tree." Satan, however, wants us to play God; so he says to us, just as he said to Adam and Eve in Genesis 3:1, "Did God really say?" Or, in other words, can you really know what he means? Isn't it just in the eye of the beholder?

Confronting the evil of relativism does not mean that people might not be mistaken about the message of a movie, but even if they are, the message is not diminished. Using proper analytical tools and Occam's razor,[9] we can know the intended message. Even without these tools, most audiences understand clearly the messages being presented to them. There is no need, therefore, to despair whenever we find people, even Christian experts, disagreeing with one another about what something means. We don't have to throw up our hands and resort to some kind of intellectual relativism that contradicts the Word of God.

## IF THE TRUMPET GIVES AN UNCERTAIN SOUND

One of our *Movieguide®* readers who understands theology sent the following letter:

> Thanks for the stand you've taken regarding the demonic assault on
> our children represented by the Harry Potter empire. As one who

works with children who have suffered all sorts of physical and sexual abuse and who has had way too many encounters with real witchcraft, I am sickened by the fact that too many in the evangelical world are sending the wrong signals to parents on this matter.

Suppose a new series of books aimed at children were introduced featuring a Larry Potter who goes to a school for male prostitutes or a Gary Potter who goes to a school for terrorists. They would, I'm confident, recognize it as poison.

The problem in my opinion is that too many dear evangelicals don't really recognize the pervasive activity of the demonic in western society and the extent to which Satan is using all sorts of media to lure children into a fascination with witchcraft. It's not that any literary references to the occult and witchcraft should be off limits. The question is whether the message regarding these abominations is that they are evil. In the case of Harry Potter, children are offered a choice between two lies: "Witchcraft is good" or "Witchcraft is make-believe." The devil doesn't really care which lie the children believe. Either way he's got their hearts. Harry Potter is not a series which includes a witch or wizard as a villain. Harry is the hero and witchcraft is good.

I'm afraid there are going to be a lot of folks wishing they had tried to swim with a millstone around their necks rather than suggesting that Harry Potter could be okay for children "as long as parents talk with them about the fact that this sort of magic is just pretend." Certainly parents need to talk with their children about these subjects, but there's no way that Christians should support EVIL or feed cleverly packaged lies to their children!

Suppose I took my boys to watch pornography so that they could be entertained like their friends but made sure to tell them that "these depictions of immoral behavior are not realistic." Suppose I sat them down to watch porn with the disclaimer: "I don't want you boys to think that sexual immorality is okay in real life. God hates real adultery! But, I'm sure he won't mind if we watch movies that make adultery and fornication and homosexuality seem like innocent fun! Just keep your immoral thoughts unrealistic, and there's no harm."

*See to it that no one takes you captive by philosophy and empty deceit, according to human tradition, according to the elemental spirits of the world, and not according to Christ. (Col. 2:8)*

*The coming of the lawless one is by the activity of Satan with all power and false signs and wonders, and with all wicked deception for those*

*who are perishing, because they refused to love the truth and so be
saved. Therefore God sends them a strong delusion, so that they may
believe what is false, in order that all may be condemned who did not
believe the truth but had pleasure in unrighteousness. (2 Thess. 9:12)*

## EFFECT OF HARRY POTTER ON TEENAGERS

A new study released by Mark Matlock and Dallas-based
WisdomWorks Ministries reveals some interesting insights regarding
teenagers and the Harry Potter franchise. The nationwide poll of teens
between the ages of thirteen and nineteen reveals that 41 percent, or
roughly 9 million teens, either have seen the first Harry Potter movie or
have read the popular books. Of those polled, 53 percent are between
the ages of thirteen and fourteen; 50 percent are A students; 49 percent
describe themselves as "stressed out"; 49 percent attend a youth group
frequently. Among the students less likely to have exposure to Harry
Potter were those with less than a B average (23 percent), African-
American teens (28 percent), and Hispanic students (31 percent).

In the face of criticism directed at Harry Potter's witchcraft themes,
one of the frequent arguments is that the stories do not encourage teen
interest in witchcraft. The WisdomWorks poll disputes that argument.
In total, 12 percent of teens exposed to Potter said they were interested
in witchcraft. Of those, 4 percent said they were a lot more interested
now, and 8 percent were a little more interested as a result of one of the
books or movies.

Mark Matlock comments:

> While this represents a minority of teens, it still accounts for about
> 5 percent of all U.S. teenagers and projects to more than a million
> students nationwide who claim that the Potter stories have made
> them more interested in witchcraft. . . . In Harry Potter, teens catch
> a vision of what they have been longing for in life. The vision is mis-
> guided, but it may give us insight into how we can "awaken" a
> yawning generation.
>
> Harry Potter believes he is an ordinary child destined to drudgery
> in the home of his adoptive aunt and uncle, until one day he is let in
> on an amazing secret: He is very special. He comes from a lineage of
> unique people and has been blessed with abilities far different from oth-
> ers. In many ways, Harry's discovery is similar to the real truth we find

in Christ. In Christ we find that we are loved and uniquely created. In God's eyes there is no one like the other, and He has made us His heirs.[10]

After Harry discovers his uniqueness, he goes to a school that any person would love to attend—a school that challenges each student and allows each one to develop his unique abilities. "This is the real intention of the church—to strengthen the believer in spirit and truth to accomplish an incredible mission that God has called us to pursue," maintains Matlock. He believes that by helping teens realize their identity and calling in Christ, the wind will be taken from the sails of the Harry Potter phenomenon. Christians will understand that the fictional vision of realizing one's own worth and uniqueness that is cast by the books and the movie is fulfilled in what they already possess in reality.

## THE HARRY DILEMMA

John Andrew Murray, who has taught cultural apologetics, notes that the church needs to distinguish between power and authority:

> Christian and non-Christian proponents of Harry Potter have sought to compare Rowling's works with C. S. Lewis's Chronicles of Narnia.
> What's the difference between Harry Potter and The Chronicles of Narnia?
> It is true that both series tell of fantasy parallel worlds involving young British children who encounter magical creatures. Both develop admirable characters and evil villains. But that is where the comparison ends.
> The difference between the two hinges on the concept of authority. From a Christian perspective, authority and supernatural power are linked.
> We can see this in Mark 2, where Jesus heals a paralytic. When Jesus first sees the paralytic He says, "Son, your sins are forgiven." This sets up the following scene:
>
> > "Now some teachers of the law were sitting there, thinking to themselves, 'Why does this fellow teach like that? He's blaspheming! Who can forgive sins but God alone?'
> > "Immediately Jesus knew . . . that this was what they were thinking . . . and He said to them, 'Why are you think-

ing such things? Which is easier: to say to the paralytic, "Your sins are forgiven," or to say, "Get up, take your mat and walk"? But that you may know that the Son of Man has authority on earth to forgive sins. . . .' He said to the paralytic, 'I tell you, get up, take your mat and go home.' He got up, took his mat and walked out in full view of them all." (Mark 2:6-12a)

Here we see a picture of the relationship between power and authority. Jesus' power flows from His authority. That's the nature of all legitimate power—it is granted and guided by authority.

When we read Rowling's series, we find that she effectively divorces power from authority. There is no sovereign person or principle governing the use of power. Magical power is gained through inheritance and learning. It is not granted by a Higher Authority, because there is no Higher Authority—at least none higher than Harry's mentor, Albus Dumbledore, and the evil Lord Voldemort.

What comes across, instead, is a kind of dualism—the idea that there are two equal, uncreated, antagonistic forces, one good and one evil, and that choosing between the two is purely a matter of personal opinion. Rowling's readers are ultimately left in a morally confused world.

In Lewis's Narnia, on the other hand, power and authority are welded together. That authority is Jesus, in the character of Aslan—creator and sovereign ruler of Narnia, son of the Emperor Beyond the Sea. Good power is power that is bestowed by Aslan and exercised in accordance with his will. We see this good power at work when Peter, Susan and Lucy use gifts bestowed on them by an agent of Aslan.

Evil power, on the other hand, is power that is seized or conjured—rather than bestowed—and exercised for selfish ends. Those who resist the temptation to use such power are commended, as was Digory in *The Magician's Nephew*. But those who wield it, such as Jadis, also in *The Magician's Nephew*, and the White Witch in *The Lion, the Witch and the Wardrobe* are eventually vanquished by Aslan.

Despite superficial similarities, Rowling's and Lewis's works are as far apart as east is from west. Rowling's work invites children to a world where witchcraft is "neutral" and where authority is determined solely by one's might or cleverness. Lewis invites them to a world where God's authority is not only recognized, but celebrated—a world that resounds with His goodness and care.[11]

## WHAT'S WRONG WITH WITCHCRAFT?

Why does God condemn witchcraft so vehemently? Because, quite simply, its practitioners try to play God and exercise power without authority over others through nefarious and invisible means. Witchcraft is rebellion against God and the order he has established. As God has said in his Word:

> *Now the works of the flesh are manifest, which are these; adultery, fornication, uncleanness, lasciviousness, idolatry, witchcraft, hatred, variance, emulations, wrath, strife, seditions, heresies, envyings, murders, drunkenness, revellings, and such like: of the which I tell you before, as I have also told you in time past, that they which do such things shall not inherit the kingdom of God.*
>
> *But the fruit of the Spirit is love, joy, peace, longsuffering, gentleness, goodness, faith, meekness, temperance: against such there is no law. And they that are Christ's have crucified the flesh with the affections and lusts.*
>
> *If we live in the Spirit, let us also walk in the Spirit. Let us not be desirous of vain glory, provoking one another, envying one another.* (Gal. 5:19-26 KJV)

# IX

# ASKING THE RIGHT QUESTIONS ABOUT FRODO AND HARRY

*Finally, brethren, whatsoever things are true, whatsoever things are honest, whatsoever things are just, whatsoever things are pure, whatsoever things are lovely, whatsoever things are of good report; if there be any virtue, and if there be any praise, think on these things.*

PHILIPPIANS 4:8 (KJV)

While most of the church is still using sixteenth-century technology to communicate the Good News, the Adversary is dropping smart bombs down the cable systems into the minds of our children and grandchildren.[1] It is not that sixteenth-century media such as books, plays, and storytelling are ineffective, but some of the mass media are more effective than others in terms of converting, motivating, and informing an audience.

What makes the entertainment media so influential today? What causes us to laugh, cry, and change our hearts and minds when we watch a movie, television program, or videotape? If we understand how the entertainment media influence us technically, we will be better equipped to use, without being abused by, the mass media.

## THE PLAY'S THE THING

Narrative story is at the heart of the influence of much of the entertainment media. William Shakespeare said, "The play's the thing wherein I'll catch the conscience of the king."[2] The essence of plays, movies, television, and even computer games[3] is the story, the most powerful genre of communications.

Jesus told stories called parables to help people understand the kingdom of God. The entertainment industry tells stories through film, television, video, CD-ROMs, radio, and the printed word. Although most of the mass media are used for storytelling, they do transmit and disseminate other forms of art and communication. Some of the media can augment the power of the story with attractive images and captivating effects. Others can involve the audience with interactive play and feedback, but the engine that drives the newscast, the computer game, and the movie is the story.

For many years the entertainment industry was so clear on the importance of the story that didactic communications were shunned. Hollywood mogul Samuel Goldwyn said, "If you want to send a message, call Western Union."[4] Goldwyn's comment ignored the fact that almost all movies and television programs—whether dramatic, news, or documentary—communicate a message.

Most Hollywood producers, directors, and executives do not intend to create art. An artist can live and die (as Van Gogh did) without having an audience. Entertainment moguls employ talented people to produce games, movies, and television programs to attract an audience so they can make money. Most movies and television programs employ art and craft elements only to attract an audience. The majority of filmmakers or television producers are not struggling artists, but court jesters, storytellers, bards, and showmen who entertain people, sometimes communicating ideas of importance and sometimes communicating ideas that rip the moral fabric of society.

Neither the media nor technology produce powerful communications. Only creative, dedicated, industrious people communicate effectively, using whatever medium is appropriate or available. Shakespeare didn't have a word processor. Yesterday talented communicators used a

pencil; today . . . television; tomorrow . . . holograms? Talent is the key
to effective communication.

## IN THE BEGINNING

A good, strong, clear premise that leads to an upbeat ending with realistic characters and exciting pacing resulting from a strong sense of jeopardy makes a story technically good and appealing to a broad audience.
Sex and violence are most often merely superficial decorations. Without
a powerful premise, sex and violence cannot make a movie or television
program good.

Sex and violence may be used to develop the plot, but usually they
are inserted to cover up a weakness in the script or as an ornament in a
lackluster story. Sex and violence will attract a few viewers, but box
office blockbusters[5] must reach a broader segment of society. They do
so by appealing to the viewers' deepest concerns and confirming their
cherished beliefs through a powerful premise that drives a redemptive,
moral story.

A story is a connected narration of real or imagined events. There
are many types of stories, including science fiction, romance, myth, fairy
tale, tragedy, and adventure. The full range of storytelling is limited only
by the human imagination; yet some key principles apply to all stories.
And all stories can be classified in terms of different genres, categories,
or sub-genres—depending on how they are constructed.

Remember Aristotle's four basic plots:
- man against man
- man against nature
- man against himself
- man against the supernatural or sub-natural

Each of these plots can be the basis of any of the many different
genres: action adventure; animation; biblical, religious, and
Christian; biography; juvenile; comedy; detective; docudrama; documentary; drama; fantasy, sword and sorcery, and science fiction;
film noir; historical; horror; kung fu or martial arts; nature and
wilderness; musical; musical comedy; mystery; romance; spy; war;
western. Each genre has its own rules and distinctives, and yet each
can use the various styles and categories common to all of them.

People at various stages of cognitive development react to different genres differently.

No matter what category or genre, stories have an internal logic driven by a basic premise. This premise works through characters in conflict to move the plot from a beginning point of attack through one or more crises to a climax that winds down into a resolution. The premise, a succinct summary statement of what the communication intends to prove, is the engine that powers the story. Characters in conflict prove the premise dramatically. United with attractive images and presented with exciting effects, the dramatic power of the premise is irresistible.

In every movie, television program, and play, the premise can be found by analyzing the story. In The Lord of the Rings trilogy Frodo must destroy an evil ring that has terrible powers in the hands of the wrong person. Good, humble heroes, with the help of providence, defeat supernatural evil. "Good triumphs over evil" is clearly the premise.

Harry Potter is a "good" sorcerer versus "bad" sorcerer tale. In the first two Harry Potter movies, Harry is a supernaturally empowered wizard who breaks the rules of Hogwarts School of Witchcraft and Wizardry in order to temporarily defeat the evil wizard Voldemort. Thus the premise is that the more powerful and more attractive wizard defeats the less powerful.

Every one of Shakespeare's plays, every good story, and even every commercial has a clear-cut premise. *King Lear* proves that blind trust leads to destruction. *The Velveteen Rabbit* tells us that love gives life to the beloved. Toothpaste commercials often claim that they give us the girl or boy of our dreams. The next television commercial you see, try to find and state the premise.

To be effective and exciting, action, not contemplation, must prove the premise. The story must *show* that good triumphs over evil, not just put those words in a character's mouth or thoughts. The elements of a premise are a subject, an active transitive verb, and an object. The verb must be active (love conquers hate) and present tense, not future or past tense, to give direction to the story. If the verb is intransitive (love is wonderful), the script will be a static photograph with no direction rather than a dynamic movie. If the verb is past tense (he loved me), the goal of the story has been achieved, and there is nothing left to prove. If the verb is future tense (he will love me), then the premise is purely specu-lative. Many well-produced films, television programs, or other media communications fail not because of the quality of the production, but because of an unclear premise, double premise, or another defect in the premise.

In a good script the environment or setting in which the action takes place must be defined in detail. The environment must be made real, even if it is far, far away in time and space. The environment and the laws that govern that environment create the illusion of reality in the story.

The style of the story must fit the premise, the environment, the characters, and the sub-genre. Style, rhythm, and tone are as important as the plot. A satiric or low ironic style may be appropriate for a detec-tive story, but not for a historic portrayal of Jesus' ministry, unless the author is attacking the gospel or has chosen Judas Iscariot's point of view.

Here again for review are the basic styles:

• In the mythic (in the classic literary sense) style, God triumphs, or the hero triumphs because of an act of God.

• In the heroic style, the hero triumphs because he or she is superior.

• In the high ironic style, the hero triumphs because of a quirk of fate.

• In the low ironic style, the hero fails because of a quirk of fate.

• In the demonic style, the hero is hopelessly overwhelmed by evil or uses evil to defeat evil.

In the mythic story The Lord of the Rings, Frodo triumphs with the help of providence and a supernatural angelic being who is good (Gandalf). In the heroic story *Harry Potter and the Sorcerer's Stone*, Harry triumphs because he is superior.

Within a style:

• To shock, the script must make the incredible credible.

• To create irony, the audience's assumptions must be contrary to the outcome.

• To create a paradox, logic must be contradicted by fact.

• To create satire, the normal is exaggerated.

• To create suspense, withheld information must confront the desire to know.

In a good script the characters must be well defined. There may be two apostles, two tax collectors, or two thieves, but one must be different from the other. They must contrast with each other so that they will move the story along. This contrast must be inherent in their character, which is revealed through their dialogue and actions. As the story progresses from beginning to end, each character grows and changes. This growth process is often referred to as the "character arc," because it can be graphed as a curve in the same way as a plot.

The protagonist, who is not necessarily the hero, is the driven, driving subject of the premise, who forces the conflict that moves the story to its conclusion. This person knows what he or she wants and will act to get it. Not only does the protagonist want something badly enough to act, but he or she will go after it until either successful or completely defeated in the process.

The antagonist opposes the protagonist's efforts to fulfill his or her goals. He or she reacts against the action of the subject. Depending on the outcome determined by the premise, the antagonist must change for the protagonist to reach his or her goal, or the protagonist must change in the face of the opposition.

To capture an audience, a story must have the right point of attack. That point is the moment in time and space when the protagonist is at a critical turning point. He or she must act to achieve the goal, thereby starting the action of the premise. Rather than ramble, looking for a place to begin, the story must start at the moment when the conflict begins, when the protagonist acts to achieve his or her goal. This moment occurs when circumstances and motivation force the protagonist to act. He or she acts out of necessity because something extremely important is at stake, such as love, survival, health, or honor. It could be a misfortune that has befallen the hero (Harry Potter's parents have been killed by the villain who wants to enact revenge on Harry for taking away the villain's power). It could be a call for help that the protagonist answers (Gandalf asks Frodo to take the evil ring to the kingdom of the elves to keep the ring out of the villain's clutches). This point could be where the protagonist has made a decision, has reached a turning point, or where something important is suddenly at stake. Whatever precipitated this moment often has already occurred when the story begins.

A good story builds through rising conflict, a series of conflicts, each building in intensity on the previous conflict until the climax is reached and the premise is proved. Each conflict moves the story forward through action and reaction, attack and counterattack, which cause change, growth, and new conflict until the premise is proved.

In order to attract an audience, storytellers must appeal to people's needs. These needs are expressed by desires. We have physical needs—for food, clothing, shelter, procreation, or survival (*Castaway*); security needs or personal protection from danger, deprivation, or accidents (*Driving Miss Daisy*); social needs—for love, community, or home (The Lord of the Rings and *Spy Kids*); self-esteem needs—for respect, productivity, or recognition (*Antz* and *Dead Poets Society*); self-fulfillment needs—for success or accomplishment (Harry Potter, *Babe*, and *Wall Street*); and most of all spiritual need, which can manifest itself as the desire for any or all of the above mentioned but in fact is a desire for communion with God, for "man does not live by bread alone" (Matthew 4:4 NIV) (*Chariots of Fire, Evelyn*, and *Dead Man Walking*).

Even so, pandering to people's needs alone will not make the story good or entertaining. All the elements of good storytelling must be in place, or even the most expensive action entertainment production will fall flat on its face. As Lajos Egri, author of the quintessential book on dramatic writing, said:

> A play [or movie] can be judged before it reaches actual production. First, the premise must be discernible from the beginning. We have a right to know in what direction the author is leading us. The characters, growing out of the premise, necessarily identify themselves with the aim of the play. They will prove the premise through conflict. The play must start with conflict, which rises steadily until it reaches the climax. The characters must be so well drawn that, whether or not the author has declared their individual backgrounds, we can make out accurate case histories for each of them.[6]

## BEYOND THE FRINGE

The images in the visual media and the special effects help to capture and influence an audience. For movies and television programs, success depends on premise, image, sounds, music, and effect. In other words, the visual and audio information in the production work together to create an image in mass media. People remember about 60 percent of the visual information and 40 percent of the audio information.

In research on the relative influence of the visual and the audio, the producers of *Sesame Street* showed a test audience comprised of people of all ages an animated short about an ant and an elephant with the sound track informing the audience that the ant could not grow to the size of an elephant because the ant's external skeleton would not sustain such weight, while the animated picture showed the ant growing to the size of the elephant and then exploding. After watching the short, the test audience was asked if an ant could grow to be as big as an elephant. Over 90 percent of the test audience said "yes" because the ant's growth portrayed in the visual animation was so much more powerful than the audio.

Image includes not only the pretty people and interesting characters in the production but also the environment in which the story is set. The environment has an immense impact on the audience. Because every communication excludes what it does not include, its omissions create powerful secondary messages in the mind of the audience.

Movies, television, and the electronic audio media are more prone to willful distortion of the real world than other media because such distortion is easy to do and because the tampered product appears to be the truth. Editing, close-ups, shadow shots, reverse shots, and other conscious camera techniques can distort reality.

The State University of New York researched the impact of television on children and found that the background environment of a television program had a tremendous impact on the worldview of the children. One little girl said she wanted to be a doctor when she grew up. When asked why, she did not answer that she felt called to heal or help others; rather, she wanted a big house with a pool, a yacht, and money to travel. The environment in which the doctors were placed on television conditioned her image of them, not the reality of medical practice.

Since a camera excludes everything beyond its field of view, television journalism is technically biased in its reporting; yet the viewer will interpret what he sees as the truth. During my (Ted's) junior year at Dartmouth College, a minor student takeover of the administration building occurred. In the middle of the night, a friend woke me to say that the National Guard was evacuating the administration building. The landscape was empty except for a few observers, a handful of National Guardsmen, the thirty students who had occupied the building, and the television news crew. However, the next day on the news, the operation looked like a major military maneuver. Frightened alumni and parents from all over the country phoned the college. The TV news team had shot the scene so tightly in the midst of the small crowd that the event looked larger and more important than it actually was. The camera had completely distorted the environment where the protest had taken place.

Gerry Mander approaches the real world on television from a humorous perspective:

> There is a widespread belief that some things on television are 'real' and some things are not real. We believe the news is real. Fictional programs are not real.
>
> Talk shows are real, although it is true they happen only for television, and sometimes happen some days before we see them.
>
> Are historical programs real? Well, no, not exactly.
>
> Our society assumes that human beings can make the distinctions between what is real and what is not real, even when the real and not real are served up in the same way, intercut with one another, sent to us from many different places and times and arriving one behind the other in our houses, shooting out of a box in our living rooms straight into our heads.[7]

How many Americans during World War II realized that much of the war footage they saw was shot in Hollywood? How many people in Great Britain realized that an actor was presenting some of Prime Minister Winston Churchill's most inspiring speeches over the radio?

To understand how the mass media influence us, we need to know that each medium has its advantages and disadvantages. An oft-quoted ancient Chinese proverb tells us, "A picture is worth a thousand words." If, however, we want to communicate the true nature of some person, event, or thing, then a few words, such as "the Word was made flesh and dwelt among us,"[8] says more than a thousand pictures.

Each medium can be seen primarily as a communications tool,[9] capable of accomplishing one or more communications functions. A tool is neither good nor bad. That is determined by how we use it. When we use a tool to perform a function for which the tool is intended, it performs well. For instance, a screwdriver is very useful for driving screws; it is of some value in scraping paint off the side of a house; it is of very little value when used to hammer a nail; it is of no value in gripping a nut (under normal circumstances).

The screwdriver is neither good when used to repair a church artifact nor bad when used to stab someone. Rather it is the person using the screwdriver who is responsible for the good or the bad, and the same is true of the various media of communications.

## DESCRIBING THE ELEPHANT

Many parents primarily look at the entertainment media in terms of the amount of sex, violence, nudity, and profanity, while many children just look at the entertainment media in terms of the rhythm, action, adventure, and special effects. So parents and children tend to talk *at* each other about the entertainment media, not *to* each other. A father might say to his son, "Did you hear the horrible lyrics in that music?" The son might reply, "No, but did you hear the riff, the rhythm, and the beat?"

Children are not immune to the messages in the mass media, but the syntactical elements of those messages influence them. Try asking a younger child what he or she is watching on television. Quite often the child will say, "I don't know." Ask the child what the program is about, and often he or she will repeat, "I don't know." However, pay attention to the child's actions, and you will often see him or her mimicking the behavior on the screen. Or later the child will ask for a product advertised with the program.

One mother was overjoyed that her young son loved Harry Potter and watched it over and over. It was clear that he did because he refused to obey anything she asked him to do.

## THUMBS UP

One set of keys to media literacy is to teach your children to analyze the mass media product by deciphering, decoding, and detecting meaning in it and then to compare and evaluate that meaning with a biblical worldview. Once they learn the right questions to ask, you can help your children broaden their perspective and develop discernment through reviewing, critiquing, and reporting on what they see and hear. The entertainment media are loaded with messages. Learning how to discover these messages helps you appreciate the movies and television programs you watch, the games you play, the music you listen to, and the mass media information sources on which you rely.

Asking the right questions requires media literacy and a working knowledge of how the medium in question communicates and entertains. Biblical discernment comes from comparing the messages you discover from the questions you ask with Christian worldview standards and principles.

There are two types of questions:

I. Ascertainment questions—which help us isolate elements, evidence, meaning, point of view, and worldview in a mass media product.

II. Discernment questions—which help us to compare the answers to our ascertainment questions with biblical standards.

## QUESTIONS TO HELP YOU MAKE WISE MEDIA CHOICES

The discernment process can be broken down into nine basic questions:

1. What kind of role models are the main characters?

2. Do the moral and spiritual statements and themes agree with a biblical worldview?

3. Are real consequences to sin exposed?

4. How are relationships and love portrayed?

5. How are Christians, religion, the church, the family, and God portrayed?

6. Does the language honor God and show respect for people?

7. If violence is included, how is it presented?

8. How much and what kind of sexual activity is implied and/or depicted?

9. How appropriate is this material for my family and me?

We will look briefly at those elements that make up powerful dramatic entertainment. These questions will help you look beneath the surface of a media product to determine whether you and God's Word writ-ten[10] agree with the messages the product communicates. A solid knowl-edge of Scripture, the wisdom that comes from a fear of the Lord, and the understanding that comes from a personal knowledge of Jesus Christ are all essential to a Christian worldview. It is this view that we want to bring to bear on the media we evaluate.

This is a call to action, including active viewing and listening. We must stimulate children to interact with the entertainment media rather than simply absorb its messages. We must discern the subtle ways in which seemingly innocuous material molds our thinking. We can do this by try-ing to explain its elements to others. This process is especially important for Christian parents to consider when communicating with their children.

For the reasons stated in the introduction, we will focus on movies and videos, including Harry Potter and Lord of the Rings, but the prin-ciples apply and are easily adapted to other media.

## ELEMENTAL AND EVIDENTIARY QUESTIONS

The first set of questions are known as elemental and evidentiary because they deal with elements of mass media products that are easily ascertained. Most of these questions help us to find out facts about mass media products about which most thinking people will agree. It should be clear after reviewing the questions that there are many others we can and should ask in order to be media literate and to discern between the good and the bad.

As you ask your child these questions after watching a movie, set a tone that supports the child's responses and creative impressions of the story. Be prepared for an animated discussion.

*Ascertainment question: Who is the hero or heroine?*

This is usually the easiest question for anyone, including children, to answer about a movie, television program, computer game, stage play, book or story. Of course, in some modern literature the reader has to realize that he is the hero (or the hero doesn't exist), or the reader must probe beyond the character's name to find out his characteristics. Then this question becomes much more complex.

Rather than talking about the main character, whom most would consider the hero or heroine, many dramatists[11] point out the character who forces the action, the protagonist. From a dramatist's point of view, the villain, such as Judas in the Passion story, can be the protagonist if he forces the action, whereas the hero, Jesus, may be the antagonist because he opposes the protagonist. Even so, our main character, in this case Jesus, remains the hero because he triumphs over his opponent(s).

For our purposes, we can conclude that in most cases, especially as far as popular entertainment is concerned, the hero or heroine is the main character, the focus of the story. Using this insight, most children can find the hero in most media products. However, they also need to look at the hero's physical characteristics, background, psychological characteristics, and religious characteristics.

As a guide to the impact a hero has on a story, here is a reminder of the five traditional literary styles:

• In the mythic style, such as The Lord of the Rings, God triumphs, or Frodo the hero triumphs because of an act of God and the help of supernatural forces from God.

• In the heroic style, such as Harry Potter, the hero triumphs because he or she is superior.

• In the high ironic style, such as *Forrest Gump*, the hero triumphs because of a quirk of fate or circumstances.

• In the low ironic style, such as *Death of a Salesman*, the hero fails because of a quirk of fate or circumstances.

• In the demonic style, which includes not only many horror films but also psychological movies and political films such as *The Diary of Anne Frank*, the hero is hopelessly overwhelmed by evil or wields evil to fight evil.

In Harry Potter, Harry was born special, although for many years he did not know it. This time of unknowing gives Harry a tendency to be secretive, to disobey, and even to lie.

Frodo, on the other hand, is a humble everyman who triumphs because of a higher grace manifest in the supernatural beings, such as Gandalf, who help him. (Gandalf, by the way, is not a human wizard but more of an angelic being with supernatural powers given to him by the Creator.) Frodo understands that he is not gifted in some special way, but he undertakes his quest because it is the right thing to do. His commitment to do the right thing and his faith in the greater good give him the ability to triumph.

*Discernment question: What kind of a role model is the hero or heroine?*

After locating the hero or heroine in the entertainment product and identifying the person's character traits, we need to discern whether he or she is a worthy role model. It is not safe to assume that the heroes of today's movies are the positive role models we want for our impressionable children. Even where the premise is positive and the morals in the entertainment product reflect a Christian worldview, we must ask the question: Does the hero meet biblical standards for a role model?

Although he has many good qualities, Harry Potter's lying, vengefulness, disobedience, and involvement in the occult set him against the biblical model of a righteous hero. Furthermore, Harry has supernatural occult powers. Every human child is created by God with unique, sometimes brilliant, talents and "gifts," and every child who comes to know Jesus Christ as Lord and Savior is filled with his Holy Spirit and the gifts that the Holy Spirit bestows on him or her. These gifts are not the same as the supernatural, paranormal powers of Harry and his friends. In contrast to Harry, Frodo is a humble, loyal, honest hobbit, warts and all, who succeeds by grace and mercy, with help from his faithful companion, Sam. Thus, while both Harry and Frodo encounter many obstacles and challenges that test their character, stamina, and strength, one hero succeeds by using evil means, witchcraft, but the other hero succeeds by holding to biblical values.

*Subsidiary discernment questions:*

• What kind of obstacles and/or challenges does the hero face, and how does he try to overcome them?

• If the hero is not a moral character, how would the story change if he were?

• How would you tell the story from another character's viewpoint?

• Do you know anyone like the hero or heroine?

• Is there a character in the Bible like the hero or heroine? Who is it? What is that person's story?

*Ascertainment question: Who is the villain?*

As in the case of the hero or heroine, we need to identify the villain and his or her character traits. In most entertainment products, the villain is easy to identify, but there are exceptions.

In the first two Harry Potter books and movies, the initial villains are Harry's nonmagic Muggle relatives, who are very cruel to Harry, but the real villain is the wizard Voldemort. Harry's Muggle relatives are a middle-class family living in England, and they often act in an unloving and repulsive manner. Children need to look at all the attributes of a character to see what kind of individual he is supposed to be, including his religious background. Voldemort is a well-defined villain who is rotten to the core.

In The Lord of the Rings, Saruman and Sauron are clearly evil in the classic biblical sense of Lucifer. That is, they are filled with pride, greed, and envy.

Once we have identified the villain, we should list his or her character traits in the same manner as with the hero or heroine. We will want to list physical characteristics, background, psychological characteristics, and religious characteristics.

*Discernment question: What message does the character of the villain communicate?*

As Christians, we need to analyze the character of the villain to determine whether he, she, or they are being used to attack a religious, biblical worldview. If so, we may want to protest this anti-Christian bigotry, and certainly we should not support it at the box office.

*Ascertainment question: How much violence is in the mass media product?*

It is important to assess the violence because of the critical influence of violence on children and susceptible individuals. Many contemporary movies and television programs push the limits.

Kenneth Turan, renowned movie reviewer for the *Los Angeles Times*, noted in his November 15, 2002, review of *Harry Potter and the Chamber of Secrets* that the "New 'Harry Potter' may leave viewers bewitched, but bothered and bewildered as well, with its emphasis on the gruesome." He continued:

> *Harry Potter and the Chamber of Secrets* is deja vu all over again, and while that is a cliché, nothing could be more appropriate. It's likely that whatever you thought of the first production—pro or con—you'll likely think of this one. Still, even partisans of *Harry Potter and the Sorcerer's Stone* may well be put off by parts of the new film.
>
> *Chamber of Secrets* displays such zeal for re-creating the book's

more grotesque aspects, from man-eating spiders to venom-dripping monster serpents, that it is sure to rattle the cages of the smallest viewers, sending them under their seats if not out of the theater.

For the Harry Potter novels have a kind of magic that it is beyond the powers of these films to duplicate. The darkness that invades *Chamber of Secrets* underlines how well the books managed to exactly balance good and evil, dark and light, so that within their pages you seemed to be experiencing both at the same time. Not so here.

Because *Chamber of Secrets* can't seem to get the balance right, it ends up broadly overdoing things on both ends of the spectrum. The film's scary moments are too monstrous and its happy times have too much idiotic beaming, making the film feel like the illegitimate offspring of *Alien* and *The Absent-Minded Professor*.

The first two Lord of the Rings movies had action violence sufficient for their PG-13 ratings (the Harry Potter movies were PG!), but the violence was not excessively gruesome in either movie, though the Lord of the Rings movies contained some strong swordplay.

*Discernment question: How is the violence presented in the mass media product?*

The heart of drama is conflict, and the ultimate conflict ends in violence. As you may realize, the Bible is full of violence, and the gospel story has one of the most violent scenes imaginable—the crucifixion of Jesus Christ. So violence in the entertainment media is not always bad; sometimes it is necessary. It is, however, critical to protect young children from such violence and to identify how it is presented so you can discern whether it is necessary and furthers the good and the true. Be aware also that the visual depiction of violence usually has a stronger impact than violence depicted in the written word.

Ron Maxwell, director of *Gettysburg*, said that while violence was essential to the storyline of the movie, he purposely avoided pornoviolence with its excessive blood, guts, and gore. His discretion made *Gettysburg* a better movie that could reach a broader audience.

The most effective stand you can make against media violence is to know before you go by reading *Movieguide®* magazine or visiting its website at www.movieguide.org and then to avoid movies with such material. Since teenagers are the most likely to attend these types of movies, it is important to help them understand why they need to make godly choices before they use any of the modern mass media.

*Discernment question: How is love portrayed?*

The beauty of God's love is wonderful; yet most movies reduce love to one-night sexual relationships, tedious ordeals, eternal battles, or homosexual coupling. This desecration of love should be an anathema to God's people.

Many horror movies capture an audience by luring them with the thought of forbidden lust such as necrophilia (fornication with the dead) and bestiality (fornication with animals). However, these movies can also serve as moral, social, psychological, and spiritual warnings about evil and sinfulness.

The most memorable and most profitable movies are usually carefully crafted character studies portraying love in a wholesome, biblical, uplifting light, such as *The Sound of Music, Finding Nemo, Beauty and the Beast, Tender Mercies, Sense and Sensibility*, and *My Big Fat Greek Wedding*.

Both The Lord of the Rings and Harry Potter have positive portraits of relationships between the sexes.

*Ascertainment question: How much sex is in the mass media product?*

In 1995 thirty-six movies were produced that had excessive sexual content. These films earned on average less than $1 million at the box office. Two of the biggest budget Hollywood sex films, *Showgirls* and *Striptease*, bombed at the box office and lost millions of dollars despite mammoth advertising campaigns. In the last seven years, movies with very strong moral and/or Christian content made more than three to six times as much money on average as movies with excessive and/or extremely graphic sexual content. Since the average Hollywood movie costs $89.6 million to produce and market, one has to wonder why the industry continues to try to force such products on the public. These movies may garner the applause of the secular critics and film festivals around the world, but they do not get much of an audience.

Neither The Lord of the Rings or the Harry Potter movies have excessive sex.

*Discernment question: How is the family portrayed?*

The Bible is very clear about the importance of the family. This institution is the local point of God's economy and governance. God created the family and ordained it as a basic unit of government along with self-government, the church, and civil government. Contemporary movies that build up the family, such as the pro-life, pro-family, pro-marriage, pro-fatherhood movie *Father of the Bride*, are rare.

Instead, today's movies tend to lift up homosexuality, promote free love, tear down marriage, portray motherhood as psychopathic, and show husbands and dads as irresponsible. These types of movies attack the basic building block of our society. In The Lord of the Rings (PG-13) movies, the family is portrayed in a positive way.

In the Harry Potter (PG) movies, Harry's family is mean, selfish, demanding, and generally rotten. So he finds a home away from his family at Hogwarts School of Witchcraft and Wizardry, with people who are like him in their special powers of witchcraft and wizardry.

*Ascertainment question: Are religion, the church, people of faith, and/or Christians in the mass media product?*

Being able to identify religious elements is an extremely important aspect of discerning viewing. Religion is alive and well in the entertainment media, especially on prime time network fiction television, but that religion is not the predominantly Christian faith of our founding fathers. It is instead a blend of materialism, consumerism, gnosticism, eroticism, hedonism, naturalism, humanism, cynicism, stoicism, the cult of violence (which used to pay homage to the war god Mars), and a multitude of other modern variations on pagan practices. These religions, many of which can trace their roots back to long-discredited ancient cults, have their rituals, beliefs, values, signs, metaphysics, cosmologies, and ultimate meanings played out with ritualistic regularity on programs, in commercials, and in music videos. On any given night on television we may find happy Hollywood stars touting the virtues of astrology or Madonna embracing a religious statue that comes alive.

*Discernment question: How are religion, Christians, and the church portrayed?*

All too often in contemporary movies religion, individual believers, and the church are portrayed as evil, weak, insincere, obsequious, or foolish.

Faith, hope, and love are positive forces in all the Lord of the Rings movies, as is the guiding of a divine providence. People who object to witchcraft, which would include Christians, are portrayed extremely negatively in the Harry Potter movies.

*Subsidiary discernment questions:*

• Does one or more of the characters play the role of God?

• Did you see anything supernatural? Who was the source: God or Satan? Or were you not sure? (Ask God to show you.)

• Does good win over evil?

• Does the winning side use spiritual power not from God? (Remember, if supernatural power is not from God, it is demonic. Frequent exposure tends to bring unquestioning acceptance; so be careful.)

• Are magic, spells, fortune telling, spiritism (contacting the spirit world or functioning as a medium between the living and the dead, as in *Ghost*) presented as a helpful means to happy living? Might they build a dangerous fascination with paganism and a desire to experiment?

*Ascertainment question: How is the world or the environment in which the story takes place portrayed?*

The environment in which a story, song, or entertainment takes place has an immense impact on the audience. Editing, close-ups, reverse shots, and other camera techniques can distort the meaning of a scene and the way we look at the world. In other words, the camera does lie. To understand how the media influence us by excluding material, look through the viewfinder of a camera and note how you can completely change the message of a scene by what you include and what you exclude. Let your children do the same, and you will help them to develop a critical media literacy skill.

The entertainment industry often distorts the way we look at the world. The next time you watch a movie, video, or television program, pay close attention to how the world or environment in which the story takes place is portrayed. Although the environment may not be the focus of your attention as you watch or listen to most media products, the setting will send distinct messages that influence how you look at the world and the subject matter of the entertainment product.

*Subsidiary ascertainment questions: Where did the story take place? How do you know?*

Children need to be aware that movies are staged—that props and scenery are used to set a story in a particular time and place. These questions help determine if your child realizes that, say, a horse and carriage signal that a story is set in the past. When children notice details, movie viewing will be a richer experience.

*Subsidiary ascertainment question: What special effects were used to create the setting and environment?*

This question helps demystify the entertainment media product so that children can see that it is pretend—that it is all created. Children can be unsettled by even seemingly innocent things; so it is important to emphasize that some movies, television programs, and other mass media products are fantasy.

If your child is very young, you might ask questions like:

• How do you think they made that character fly without getting hurt?

• What pretend things were the characters doing?

A lot of young children want to duplicate what they see; so it is wise to point out to them what is not real.

*Subsidiary ascertainment question: How is language used?*

Closely related to the environmental ascertainment and discernment question is the question of how language is used in a mass media product. A definitive study by Professor Timothy Jay, "Cursing in America,"[12] found that only 7 percent of American people curse on the job and only 12 percent in their leisure time; yet many movies and television programs would lead us to believe that Americans curse all the time because these media are so full of profanity and obscenity. It may be rare to hear cursing in your local grocery store or mall, but turn on your TV, radio, or go to the movies, and you will hear a constant barrage of cursing.

One school of Marxist thought considered language as a weapon with which to attack the bourgeois society in which we live.[13] Several filmmakers belong to this school.

In the years *Movieguide*® has been tracking language in movies, we have found that the more foul language included in a movie, the worse it will do at the box office.

*Discernment question: How are government and business portrayed?*

This question belongs as a subset of the question, "How is the world portrayed?" Because so many movies attack conservative governments and promote socialism and communism, it behooves us to pay close attention to the way a movie portrays government and business. Furthermore, to really analyze the worldview being foisted upon us by a motion picture, we should also ask, How is private enterprise portrayed in the movie?

The Lichter, Rothman, and Lichter studies[14] show that the vast majority of those involved in the entertainment industry advocate socialism. In this form of government, the state, not God, is the savior of mankind.

At the very root socialism and communism oppose God's Law, the Ten Commandments, particularly the first, since the state is elevated to a position higher than God; the eighth, because the redistribution of property by the state is stealing from those who are forced to give up their property against their will; and the tenth, because the whole premise of socialism and communism is based on envy or coveting what belongs to someone else. A movie that lifts up the state as savior and attacks the individual and his God-given rights is promoting a very anti-Christian worldview. Asking how government, business, and private enterprise are portrayed will help us cut through the hidden political agendas that occur in too many movies and television programs.

*Discernment question: How is history treated in the media product?*

Any familiarity with world history will convince us that those who forget the past are doomed to repeat it. When the media revise the past to suit their worldview, that is a very serious issue for the future of our civilization.

Much revisionism has been devoted to whitewashing the Holocaust of European Jews during World War II. Those who deal in this area of revisionism are anxious to remove the memory of the Holocaust from the annals of history by claiming that the gas chambers could not have killed so many people and that the death camps were actually work camps with good sanitary conditions.

While *Schindler's List* accurately portrays the horror of the Holocaust, *The English Patient* whitewashes the real history of its Nazi hero, extols adultery, and promotes euthanasia.

Any thinking person understands the threat of revising history to remove the memory of the Holocaust, but few object to the wholesale revision of the history that supports our republican democracy and

Christian heritage. Historian Catherine Millard has chronicled the removing of Christian quotes and information from our national monuments by the U.S. Park Service and the removal of the Christian writings of our Founding Fathers from the Library of Congress in her book *The Rewriting of America's History* (Horizon). Her book gives a frightening look at how the revisionists are trying to remove any trace of Christianity from our society.

## WORLDVIEW QUESTIONS

We move out of the evidentiary area toward the philosophical perspectives that the mass media feed us. In order to discern meaningful biblical agendas, we need first to distinguish between the differing worldviews and man's relation with himself, his world, and his God.

The term *discernment* has a much deeper meaning than identifying discrepancies between "good" and "bad" viewing, which is to see the differences between the two elements and to make an educated decision. We are here to build discernment, and discernment involves our entire process of thinking, feeling, and knowing so that we are able to recognize pieces of media or information as moral, ethical, and holy or as information that does not follow the laws of God and his plan for our lives.

The second set of questions that we will ask are worldview questions because they deal with the underlying elements of the mass media product. We can determine the worldview by looking at the dynamic interfaces between the evidentiary elements. These elements help us to understand the philosophical and theological messages that the product communicates and are critical to making discerning decisions.

*Ascertainment question: What is the premise of the movie?*

If you understand the premise, then you understand the ultimate message the product communicates to the audience. The premise drives the story to its conclusion. Whether or not the audience is conscious of the premise, it implants its message in their minds.

The storyline logically proves the premise. If the premise is that "good triumphs over evil," then the storyline has to tell in a logical manner how the good hero triumphs over the evil villain, or the story will fail to capture the audience.

Without a clear-cut premise, no idea is strong enough to carry a story through to a logical conclusion.[15] The characters will not come to life. A badly worded or false premise will force the movie-maker[16] to fill space with irrelevant material. A mass media product with more than one premise is confusing because it tries to go in more than one direction. A premise that says too much is ambiguous and therefore says nothing. A premise that does not take a position is ambivalent and therefore says nothing.

In most cases, a mass media-maker will not be able to produce a successful entertainment product based on a premise that he or she does not believe. No one premise expresses the totality of universal truth, and every premise is limiting. For example, poverty does not always lead to crime, but if the mass media-maker has chosen the premise that poverty leads to crime, he or she must prove it.

Here are some sample premises:
- God's love triumphs over death (*Dead Man Walking*).
- Great faith triumphs over death (*Lady Jane*).
- Love conquers death (*Romeo and Juliet*).
- Great faith triumphs over despotism (*Braveheart*).
- Ruthless ambition destroys itself (*Macbeth*).
- Strength defeats evil (*Rambo*).
- Cunning defeats evil (*Alien*).
- Love and laughter defeat fear and evil (*Monsters, Inc.*).
- God triumphs over self-centeredness (*The Preacher's Wife*).
- God's call triumphs over bondage (*Trip to Bountiful*).

The premise can be found by analyzing the story. In *Driving Miss Daisy*, an elderly woman has alienated all those around her. Motivated by his Christian faith, her black chauffeur makes the effort to help her, ignoring her cruelty and demeaning barbs. In the end she recognizes that he is her only friend. This heart-warming story has the incredibly powerful premise that Christian virtues bring reconciliation and love into an old woman's life.

Finding the premise will help your children develop cause-and-effect thinking, which is so important in understanding a story. Another way of finding the premise is to ask: Why did the story end the way it did?

*Discernment question: Does the premise agree with, or conflict with, a biblical worldview?*

If the premise is not consistent with a biblical worldview, then you need to question the message the product is leaving in the minds of the audience.

The premise of The Lord of the Rings resonates with a Christian, biblical worldview, whereas the premise of Harry Potter offers a pagan, occult worldview.

*Ascertainment question: How is the premise solved?*

It is quite possible that the premise can agree with the biblical worldview, but the way that premise is solved may be anti-Christian, immoral, or evil. If that is the situation, then the media product is problematic viewing for Christians committed to their faith.

In many movies good triumphs over evil but only by means of a kind of magic. So while the premise ("good triumphs over evil") agrees with the biblical worldview, the method by which the premise is solved (magic) is unbiblical. These movies are suspect for anyone who does not recognize the dangers of magic. If the magic were a literary device to point away from the manipulation of the supernatural for personal gain and toward God's grace, as in The Chronicles of Narnia and The Lord of the Rings, then that redemptive aspect of the story would make the movie more acceptable.

*Subsidiary ascertainment question: What is the plot of the media product, or what is it about?*

Part and parcel of identifying the premise is to be able to describe the plot. To do so you need to answer the five "W's" and the "H": who, what, where, when, why, and how. Always attempt to identify in the film as many of these as you think need to be answered. Often it is a good idea to try to do this in one or two sentences.

Describing the plot will help your children understand stories. This straightforward question shows whether your children understand a movie's main ideas and will also prompt children to recall details and incidents in sequence, two important thinking skills. Education specialists stress the importance of asking questions deeply and not widely— to explore knowledge, comprehension, application, analysis, synthesis, and evaluation.

*Subsidiary discernment question: What images/sounds would you say best summarize the media product?*

A sound-image schema can help you discover recurring themes, motifs, and underlying principles. Ask your children to state one sound or image that relates to the story and discuss different suggestions from the family.

Sometimes sounds and images recite themselves unconsciously over and over in the mind like an unwanted mantra. (Of course, no Christian wants any mantra, especially one placed in our minds by a media product.)

Children constantly repeat songs from commercials such as McDonald's advertisements. Ask them to think about the songs and what they mean. Most children will come to the conclusion that they do not want to be singing songs that manipulate them.

Only when these ideas are presented to the conscious mind can we make decisions about their appropriateness in our hearts and heads. We can choose to accept the song and dance or refuse the negative images.

*Ascertainment question: What are the moral statements in the media product?*

*Discernment question: Do the moral statements agree or conflict with a biblical worldview?*

Besides having a premise that drives the story to its logical conclusion, many media products make one or more moral statements. The Lord of the Rings makes statements that humility, loyalty, and commitment are to be valued, there are some good things worth fighting for, and there is a divine plan. Harry Potter has the themes that disobeying rules is praiseworthy if successful, family is restrictive, and playing tricks on others is justified if funny.

*Ascertainment question: How is evil portrayed?*

*Discernment question: How does the portrayal of evil in the media product compare with the biblical view of evil?*

Heretical doctrine can most often be traced to an incorrect view of evil. Humanism and Romanticism see man as basically good and minimize evil and sin. New Age religions and Hinduism see evil as simply an illusion. Occultism and Satanism believe that evil is as strong as, if not stronger than, the ultimate good, who is God. That evil be presented for what it is—real, not illusory or imaginary, the negation of the good, and defeated by Jesus on the cross—will be critical to an orthodox Christian worldview.

Harry Potter portrays evil as having tremendous power and says that the hero can only succeed by participating in occult activity. The Lord of the Rings portrays evil as something that no one would want to participate in and shows that rebellion and disobedience have negative consequences.

*Ascertainment question: What is portrayed as real?*

*Discernment question: How does this portrayal compare to the biblical norm?*

This is the classic ontological question (ontology is the study of the nature of being, reality, or existence): That is, how is the very nature of being, which is reality, presented in the mass media product?

For Christians and Jews the biblical view is that we live in a real world, created by the real God, wherein there are real problems, pain, and suffering that we cannot ignore or wish away. For those of us who are Christians, the Creator God has saved us from real evil, sin, and death through the real death and resurrection of his Son, Jesus the Christ, who was really God and really man. Any other ontology or view of the nature of being denies the gospel.

Every movie has an ontology whether the producer, writer, or director knows it or not. The first two Harry Potter books and movies present an occult ontology filled with magical thinking that is contrary to the Word of God, though they have a moral conclusion. The Lord of the Rings has an ontology where there are real consequences for Frodo and the other characters' actions, real death, and real solutions that require taking responsibility.

*Subsidiary ascertainment and discernment question: How does the media product present knowledge, and how does that presentation compare with the biblical norm?*

How do we know that anything exists? This question is often phrased, How do you know that a tree fell in the forest if no one, including yourself, sees it?

Christians and Jews believe in a real epistemology, which means that they know because God tells them. He has told us that his laws govern all creation, including the forest; so we know that the life and death of trees occurs because trees are subject to his laws. The Lord of the Rings has this real epistemology.

Many media products, including Harry Potter, take an existentialist perspective that you cannot know and therefore are trapped in an unpredictable and frightening world. Other media products that offer this perspective, such as Sartre's famous play *No Exit*, suggest that as a result life is essentially meaningless. This kind of perspective is nihilistic.

I (Tom) once ran into a professed nihilist at a philosophical discussion group between believers and nonbelievers. The nihilist happened also to be an animal rights activist, which was self-contradictory because nihilism says that the concept of moral values, including animal rights, is meaningless. When asked about this contradiction, the nihilist said that, since everything is meaningless, including the laws of logic, it did not matter if he personally chose, as a nihilist, to be an animal rights activist and to reject Christianity, because even our choices are ultimately meaningless.

Of course, this is nonsense as well as willful rebellion against the God who created him. Such a worldview is irrational, lacks mental clarity, is unbelievably egotistical, and leads to a life emptied of any ultimate significance whatsoever.

*Subsidiary ascertainment and discernment question: What is the cosmology of the media product, and how does it compare with the biblical norm?*

Christians and Jews believe God created the universe; therefore, the universe is governed by his laws of creation. Since he has informed us that he is good, we can trust those laws of creation and explore the universe with confidence.

In contrast, many media products have an evolutionary cosmology, which means that nothing is certain, and everything is ultimately pointless. Thus you need to understand the cosmology of a media product to make discerning entertainment choices.

*Ultimate ascertainment question and discernment question: What is the worldview of the product, and how does it compare with a biblical worldview?*

Developing a biblical worldview involves much more than a particular perspective or filter over a lens. Your worldview defines your approach to all areas of thought, including mass media, education, politics, religion, family, law, business, and government. It is the task of the viewer to examine the messages and assumptions that the entertainment industry imparts and to ask the kind of questions that pierce through thinking that is inconsistent with biblical principles. Parents have this opportunity to teach their children how to probe beneath these assumptions to test their truth or validity against the Word of God.

When looking at a media product, ask the basic philosophical questions:

- What is the nature of reality?
- What can we know about reality?
- What is the nature and purpose of humanity?
- How do we decide what is good or evil?
- In what does a human find value?
- What is the relationship of the individual to God? To self? To nature?
- Is truth relative or the same regardless of the era or culture?
- How does the hero live his life justly?

Every media product is a reflection and a projection of the broader culture in which we live. The entertainment industry often regards the problematic elements in their media products as problematic elements of our society as a whole.

The entertainment industry evades criticism by appealing to the First Amendment and by claiming that a media product cannot be judged out of the context of our culture. Clearly, that is false. We need to make righteous judgments and view the world through God's Word, not view God's Word through the eyes of the world. We need to be media literate and familiar with a biblical worldview and then compare the worldviews of the media products we encounter with that biblical worldview.

*Ascertainment question: Is there any redeeming value?*

A media product can have unbiblical worldviews and still be redemptive. *Nothing in Common* starts out focusing on the story of an egocentric young advertising executive who pushes everyone around and plays with every woman he meets, but ends with him giving up his job and his fast life to take care of his sick father. He makes a decision for love that costs him everything in the world's eyes but gives him back his father and a new appreciation of life.

Surprisingly, his boss lets him leave employment with the insight that "there has been only one perfect son," or so he had been told. *Nothing in Common* tells the story of a man who has been moved by the power of love from selfishness to selfless giving—a redemptive message.

It is rare that a movie has a redemptive aspect that transcends the negative elements. Some children's films such as *The Dirt Bike Kid* does because the negative parts are treated lightly, with deference and a lack of conviction as storytelling devices, while the redemptive element of love, courage, or integrity is emphasized. If a motion picture does transcend its negative aspects because of some redemptive element, then we need to be aware of the good and the bad in the movie so that we can discuss it honestly and rebut the negative elements.

## REFLECTION QUESTIONS

*Reflection question: Would you be embarrassed to sit through the movie with your parents, your children, or Jesus?*

When we are alone or with a friend we often deceive ourselves regarding the true nature of a movie (or television program). If we ignore the faults in a movie we are watching, then we will slowly be conditioned to condone, if not accept, a non-Christian point of view.

*Reflection question: What was your favorite part? Why did you like that part so much?*

Here you're guiding children to think about how the mass media product relates to real life. Most important, you're boosting a child's self-esteem. Any time you ask children their opinion, you build their confidence tremendously.

*Reflection question: If you were an actor in this movie, what character would you be?*

Children usually love to think about the character they identify with most or would most like to be. Your child's responses, of course, can give you insights into his or her wishes and concerns. Children are prone to accept role models and the underlying belief systems that these models exercise and demonstrate. In this discussion, a parent can expose worldviews and value systems that are inconsistent and even dangerous.

*Subsidiary reflection question: Would you do just what that character did, or do you think you would have done things differently?*

This question gets children thinking about the plausibility of characters' actions. It's important to invite your child to consider whether a character's action was the right choice—because sometimes mass media product-makers manipulate a character's choice just to make the story more exciting. Children should know that that kind of thing goes on in Hollywood.

*Reflection question: What did you like about the hero/heroine? What things were important to the hero/heroine? Are those things important to you?*

Get children to explore the connection between the character and their own lives. Children become aware of why they like a character—because the character made them feel good or because he or she did something they could do. Mass media products made for children often-times communicate positive values of honesty, loyalty, and so on. So, hopefully, your child will respond to your questions with answers like, "Well, she was a good friend to him and believed in him no matter what," conveying to you that your child is picking up on values. Together you can also discuss a full range of solutions to the problem this character faced and explore possible biblical remedies for future problems.

*Reflection question: What feelings did you have as you watched or listened? When did you feel sad, mad, or scared? What part of the story made your feelings change?*

Can your child identify what he or she is feeling? Does the child realize that it is the media product and the storyline that causes the feelings? It is important for parents to explore this area because children need to put a name to their feelings—especially younger children who might not know the source of their feelings. Asking children questions such as these after seeing a movie helps them identify that source.

There are many other questions we could ask to help evaluate a motion picture, but they may be boiled down to this: Would we like our loved ones to be inundated by the messages communicated by the media? If we care about others and about the Lord Jesus, we will take a stand against anything that undermines a biblical worldview and mocks our Lord and Savior Jesus Christ. Anything less than standing on his Word written denies our relationship with him.

## CONCLUSION

In previous centuries "entertainment" was a once-in-a-while experience. Someone might read aloud or play a musical instrument, or there might be an occasional visit to the theater. Today's use of the media has no relationship to those occasional happenings. It is not separate from the daily routine; it *is* the daily routine.

God's standards have not changed. His expectation for us is that we will try to bring each thought into captivity and be good stewards of the time he has given us on this earth. Bringing our thoughts into captivity is a lifelong challenge and an eternal command.

By ourselves, we can't resist the devil's schemes. However, God, who is far greater than Satan, has already won the war. When we know and follow him, he makes us "more than conquerors" in Christ.

# X

# CONCLUSION:
## SEEK WISDOM, KNOWLEDGE, AND UNDERSTANDING

*Blessed is the one who finds wisdom, and the one who gets understanding, for the gain from her is better than gain from silver and her profit better than gold. She is more precious than jewels, and nothing you desire can compare with her. Long life is in her right hand; in her left hand are riches and honor. Her ways are ways of pleasantness, and all her paths are peace.*

PROVERBS 3:13-17

Every Christian is called to know God and make him known because we love God and our neighbor. This is the essence of theology—knowing God to make him known to the lost and hurting that they might be rescued from eternal damnation. God has no grandchildren, and so it is up to us to communicate the Good News of salvation to all mankind.

Every generation is tempted to abandon this charge and turn instead to the study of man in a vain attempt to save themselves. In many countries that were vibrant centers of Christian faith and values, there is only a remnant left. Correct theology is important to help us stand firm in the free gift of salvation and to help us rescue the lost.

*Frodo and Harry: Understanding Visual Media and Its Impact on*

*Our Lives* is an introductory insight into a biblical analysis of important cultural influences. The audience for these books and movies will fall into three groups—those who seem not to be affected by them, those who react negatively, and those who will be deeply influenced, for good or ill, by them. Informed Christian parents, educators, and other believers can help each one of these audience groups come closer to knowing the truth that will set them free.

## NO OTHER GODS

Trendy dilettantes have the gall to say that movies and the other mass media products are art and that anything in the name of art is acceptable. Art, they say, is truth, and so all art is worthy of some audience.

The movie industry is a more than $30 billion a year business that appeals to people's visceral emotions to separate them from their hard-earned dollars. Much of that money comes from mass media products with a heavy dose of perverse sex and violence. Some in the entertainment industry call these "horny boy" movies because they are targeted at the hormones of teenage boys who drag their dates along so they can be desensitized to promiscuous sex and physical violence.

All of the mass media of entertainment employ some artistic elements and some communicative elements, but these elements are employed only to enhance the money-making value of the product. Art per se is not truth. It is a product of man's creativity, or, as Aristotle said, "Art is contrary to nature."

Art is sometimes truthful, sometimes lies, and often does neither. Not only should we avoid setting art apart as some holy object to be venerated, but we must also stop looking at the entertainment industry apart from God's Law as if it were beyond good and evil. Ignoring God's Law in the name of art, speech, or entertainment is the heresy of antinomianism (anti-law), which is abhorrent to God. Those who condone such lawlessness in the name of art are condoning the moral decay of our society.

Christians must resist the temptations of the world, the flesh, and the devil and stand up for what they believe. United we can influence the media elite by impacting the box office and the cash register.

## WE ARE HIS BODY

The apostle Paul said, "Now you are the body of Christ and individually members of it" (1 Cor. 12:27). God has instructed us through his apostle to stand in holy armor against the wiles of the Adversary—including immoral media. We not only have every right to unite to oppose evil communications, but we are called to rebuke such evil in the love of Christ because we care about our children and our neighbors.

## GOD IS STILL IN CONTROL

Too many moral Americans believe that in the fight against immoral entertainment, we face overwhelming odds and unassailable power. Paul Klein, former vice president of NBC, said, "Television is the most powerful force in the world today."

Not even close. Television, nuclear power, communism, capitalism, the United States, sin, Satan, man, and all other powers combined pale to shadowy insignificance when compared to the power of God: "All things were made through him, and without him was not any thing made that was made" (John 1:3). Do not despair; God is in control. Trust in him at all times.

## THE ANSWER

Jesus alone can deliver us from sin and death. Only the sword of his Spirit, his Word written, can give us victory over the evil influences of this age. He was the master of communications. His dramatic parable word pictures are as pertinent today as they were 2,000 years ago. He understood the power of communications and how ideas shape civilizations. His Word conquered one of the most powerful civilizations in history, the Roman Empire, and continues to transform the world today.

We must care enough for him and for our neighbor to communicate his gospel with power and love throughout the world and to take every thought captive for him. We must learn the principles of powerful communication so that we can communicate the gospel through the mass media of entertainment to reach every man, woman, and child with his truth.

Furthermore, we must redeem the mass media of communications so that the good, the true, and the beautiful—not vain, false, and evil imaginations—are proclaimed through the mass media of entertainment throughout the world.

In obedience to his Word written, Christians need to reclaim the media for Christ by advancing on several fronts:

• We need to raise the consciousness of Christians to impact the industry.

• We need to lobby the television and motion picture companies to observe a code of decency so they can include rather than exclude the Christian audience.

• We need to witness to and disciple those in the mass media.

• We need to produce quality programming and motion pictures.

## HELP STOP CHRISTOPHOBIA

One reason there is so little evangelism and so much ignorance about the biblical worldview is the rampant growth of Christophobia in our society. This term here refers to those who have an irrational fear of and hostility toward Jesus Christ and anything Christian. The symptoms are quite simple and insidious:

• An unhealthy fear of using the name of Jesus as anything but a profanity in public.

• A dread of discussing biblical principles in public.

• A horror that someone, including politicians and government officials, would expose or discuss his or her Christianity in public, much less put Christian principles into action.

• An aversion to using biblical standards to make decisions and to determine right and wrong in any given situation.

• A perverse fear of the Bible.

There are many more symptoms of this dysfunctional condition and many other situations where Christophobia rears its ugly head in our society. We see it all too frequently in our families, schools, media, and government institutions. For example:

• Christmas is now called Winter Holidays.

• Easter vacation is avoided by school systems, even if it means skewing school calendars to create unbalanced terms.

• Newspapers, radio stations, and television executives ask Christian writers to edit out any biblical references from their stories or scripts. Those who refuse are mocked and humiliated in print and on the public airwaves.

• Courts refuse to consider the biblical point of view.

This destructive phobia has spread throughout our culture to the extent that Christians are often the most Christophobic members of our society. These Christophobic Christians get livid when someone brings up a biblical perspective, apologize when the name of Jesus is used in reverence, complain when Christians stand together, and worry that some Christians may be wearing their Christianity on their sleeves.

Often these fearful, Christophobic Christians fret about using biblical standards to determine right and wrong. They are horrified that these standards might be applied to common "problems" such as murder, adultery, lying, sodomy, homosexuality, and the other evils condemned by the Word of God.

If this phobia continues at its current pace, it will become the most debilitating psychological aberration of our age. Christophobia causes many to hide their Christianity, others to deny it, and still others to lash out at Christians. It may even inaugurate a widespread persecution of Christians and a denial of the Christian roots of our society. History will be revised to blame Christians for all the problems in the world, and the immorality condemned by the Bible will be acclaimed as the solution to our problems.

This abnormal psychological condition must be routed out of our national psyche before it is too late. Christians must help others understand the dysfunctional aspects of this disease. We must deliver those who suffer from it by introducing them to Jesus Christ and instructing them in the wholesome benefits of the biblical worldview.

## DELIVERANCE

There is a war raging around us, but not the one on the news. Rather, the war is spiritual and is being fought for the hearts and souls of human beings. The victory in this war is only to be found in Jesus Christ.

In Christ protection from powerful evil spirits begins with the awareness of the subtle effect that other individuals, groups, and even the media often exert on us. Following such awareness, we need to recognize that God wants to deliver us from the demons of our age, and he will.

> *As for you, you were dead in your transgressions and sins, in which you used to live when you followed the ways of this world and of the ruler of the kingdom of the air, the spirit who is now at work in those who are disobedient. All of us also lived among them at one time, gratifying the cravings of our sinful nature and following its desires and thoughts. Like the rest, we were by nature objects of wrath. But because of his great love for us, God, who is rich in mercy, made us alive with Christ even when we were dead in transgressions—it is by grace you have been saved. And God raised us up with Christ and seated us with him in the heavenly realms in Christ Jesus, in order that in the coming ages he might show the incomparable riches of his grace, expressed in his kindness to us in Christ Jesus. For it is by grace you have been saved, through faith—and this not from yourselves, it is the gift of God—not by works, so that no one can boast. For we are God's workmanship, created in Christ Jesus to do good works, which God prepared in advance for us to do. (Eph. 2:1-10 NIV)*

Once Christ has saved us from the spirits of our age, we need to walk in the Spirit of God and renew our minds according to the Bible. As Paul states in his letter to the Romans (12:1-2): "I appeal to you therefore, brothers, by the mercies of God, to present your bodies as a living sacrifice, holy and acceptable to God, which is your spiritual worship. Do not be conformed to this world, but be transformed by the renewal of your mind, that by testing you may discern what is the will of God, what is good and acceptable and perfect."

In addition, if we discover compromise in our lives, we need to repent, turn away from it, and seek the Lord with all our hearts. We also need to break off any associations not of God and renounce any ungodly spirits. Then we must avoid any further spiritual oppression by staying in the Word of God daily, walking in the Spirit of God, and using the spiritual armor God has given us through Jesus Christ. Thus we can enjoy the provision Christ has made for us to walk in him and not give way to the evil that surrounds us, "for he who is in you is greater than he who is in the world" (1 John 4:4).

In all of this, it is important to remember that God is sovereign, we are more than conquerors in Jesus Christ, and God gives us the victory. In fact, this is the essence of the Good News that we need not despair and can rest and rejoice in him. "Rejoice in the Lord always; again I will say, Rejoice. Let your reasonableness be known to everyone. The Lord is at hand; do not be anxious about anything, but in everything by prayer and supplication with thanksgiving let your requests be made known to God. And the peace of God, which surpasses all understanding, will guard your hearts and your minds in Christ Jesus" (Phil. 4:4-7).

The magnificent glory of God's loving grace, which we meet in Jesus Christ, is magnified when we perceive the harsh reality of the judgment that awaits all those who reject Jesus as Lord and Savior. However, "if we confess our sins, he is faithful and just to forgive us our sins and to cleanse us from all unrighteousness" (1 John 1:9).

Delivered from the judgment they deserve, those who know his salvation cannot keep on sinning, for "no one who keeps on sinning has either seen him or known him" (1 John 3:6).

## CAST YOUR VOTE

Once we are saved, redeemed, and delivered, we need to exercise discernment in order to detect the difference between good and evil, even in movies, videos, and television programs. Discernment comes from seeking knowledge of God and understanding of God's Word. However, we need more than discernment. As one young caller said to Ted on a radio program, "I have discernment; that's why I can see these vile movies." The next step after discernment is wisdom, which means *choosing the good and rejecting the bad.*

This choice at the box office is known as patron sovereignty. Patron sovereignty has traditionally been commended by Hollywood as the right of movie patrons to determine what they want to see, or avoid, by their activity at the box office. In our free society we can again exercise our freedom to influence the motion picture industry to produce moral, uplifting movies. Despite widespread preferences that favor sex, violence and anti-Christian messages, the producers in Hollywood are ultimately concerned about the bottom line—how much money they can make at the box office. If Christians attend good films and avoid immoral films, our impact will be quickly felt in Hollywood.

The Adversary often convinces us that we are powerless—that there is not much we can do except complain, escape, or avoid something. The truth is that we have great power. We can change the nature of television and films.

## THE POWER OF THE CONSUMER

You and your family have the power to help redeem the values of the entertainment industry. The power of the consumer to stop pornography and violence is illustrated by the success of two mothers, Kathy Eberhardt and Karen Knowles. They forced Tri-Star Pictures (owned by Columbia Pictures) to pull from the theaters a grotesque movie, *Silent Night*, that had cost millions to produce. The movie is about a lunatic who dresses in a Santa Claus outfit and then rapes and chops up women in front of their frightened children.

These outraged mothers picketed the Grand Theatre in their hometown of Milwaukee, Wisconsin. They said they feared the movie might cause teenage viewers to emulate the violence in the film. They referred to the NBC-TV movie *The Burning Bed*. After it was shown in Milwaukee, a local man murdered his wife by pouring gasoline on her and lighting a match—copying the murder in the TV movie.

This protest spread from Milwaukee to Chicago, and after just a few days of protesting, Tri-Star relented and pulled the multimillion dollar release from national distribution. Two women defeated a modern Goliath simply by taking a stand.[1]

## DISCIPLE YOUR NEIGHBORS

After speaking at a large church in Atlanta, a woman named Pat Logue told me (Ted) that our biblical *Movieguide®* reviews and our "Taking Hollywood for Christ" banquet had changed her life.

She owned a successful video store and loved horror movies. One of our *Movieguide®* families (Mr. and Mrs. Robert Mikesell and their children) had witnessed to her every time they came into her store. They loaned her copies of *Movieguide®* and prayed constantly for her. As a result of their witness and the witness of others, she had come to Christ.

In 1987 the Mikesells invited Logue to the Good News "Taking Hollywood for Christ" banquet. Logue became convicted about the moral quality of the movies in her store. Suddenly she couldn't watch horror movies anymore. In fact, she could hardly watch the movies she had to put in her store.

Though she said her clientele had changed from pagans to Christians, she was appalled at what Christians were renting. God convicted her that she had to destroy the 3,000 video tapes that constituted the remaining stock of her store.

## PLEDGE ALLEGIANCE

The Legion of Decency was able to redeem Hollywood movies in 1933 because thousands of people signed a pledge not to see obscene and immoral movies. We have updated that famous pledge so that thousands of Americans can once again join together to stop the flood of obscene movies and encourage a return to wholesome entertainment. If you are willing to stand with us, please call or write, and we will send you a copy of the Concerned Americans for Moral Entertainment Pledge.

Like the Legion of Decency, *Movieguide*® is commissioned to criticize movies from a moral, biblical point of view. We make only one demand: clean movies, clean speech, and wholesome entertainment for all Americans.

We publish *Movieguide*®: *A Biblical Guide to Movies and Entertainment* every month. The publication gives a detailed review of each movie so people can choose the movies to see or to avoid. Each review provides a biblical perspective, enabling readers to discern based on a biblical worldview. *Movieguide*® also equips people to confront ungodly communications and take every thought captive for Jesus Christ.

While some Christians choose not to watch any movies, more than two-thirds of the born-again evangelical and/or charismatic Christians watch the same things non-Christians watch. And many parents have written us saying they had no idea what their sons and daughters were watching until they subscribed to *Movieguide*®. Now they talk about movies with their teenagers and discuss why they should not watch specific movies and videos. Other people thank us for making them aware of things they missed in a movie or video, which helped them be more discerning.

Movieguide® is available on the Internet and Worldwide Web at *www.movieguide.org* for those who want immediate information on movies and videotapes. It is reprinted in many Christian publications and is broadcast over the USA Radio Network. In addition, the Movieguide® television program is broadcast by more than 300 television stations and cable systems throughout the United States of America and in 215 other countries.

Many teenagers have told us they did not notice the evil in the movies until they started reading Movieguide®. Many say they turned from those films toward the Bible. Others say they gave up movies entirely.

## GOOD NEWS

GNC/CFTVC has undertaken to reestablish the church's presence in Hollywood; and, by God's grace, we are making a difference. In fact, we have seen great breakthroughs visible in the movies being released at the box office. Undergirded by the grace of God, the reasons we have had such success in Hollywood are fivefold:

• Through our extensive research we have been able to demonstrate to Hollywood executives that family films and clean mature-audience films do better at the box office.

• As the audience gets older, which it will continue to do until the year 2009, it will move to more family fare in movies and television programs.

• Many of the Hollywood executives and talent now have families and want to produce movies and programs that their families can watch.

• Many Hollywood executives and talent are now involved in their own causes, and when they claim that the media influence people politically or environmentally, they find it difficult to deny that influence with regard to violence and sexual mores.

• Many Hollywood executives and talent are coming to know Jesus Christ as Lord and Savior and are going to church.

Some of the signs of success include:

• A major movie studio turned down two anti-Christian movie projects.

• Several television and movie producers have consulted with us on their scripts and, following our advice, rewrote them to appeal to a broader audience.

• A television network and several top Hollywood producers and talent have met to strategize the production of more family films.

• Several top executives and producers met with us to learn more about broad audience movies and programs.

• To help encourage more godly movies and television programs, philanthropist Sir John Templeton appointed *Movieguide®* and Christian Film & Television Commission to present a cash Epiphany Prize for the "Most Inspiring Movie" and the "Most Inspiring Television Program."

• Doors to the most important offices in Hollywood have been opened, and evidence mounts that a powerful sea change is occurring in the entertainment industry at the very highest levels.

• The chairman of Dreamworks asked us to put together a theological board of advisors for their big-budget animated movie *Prince of Egypt*.

Though pessimistic voices say the golden age of Christianity is over and suggest that the Christian faith is being replaced by Islam and other beliefs, Christianity is the world's fastest growing religion. It is growing faster than the world's population. The Lausanne Statistics Task Force reports that the ratio of non-Christians to Bible-believing Christians now stands 6.8 to one, the lowest ratio in history. The evangelical movement worldwide is growing three times faster than the world's population.

While the mass media of entertainment tries to associate Christians with rednecks and rubes, the Barna Research Group says church attendance increases with education.

## WHAT WILL HAPPEN?

We will continue to make an impact on the entertainment industry, encouraging production of positive, morally uplifting films and television programs. We will continue to help the heads of the entertainment companies understand the issues involved. And we will help more Christians develop discernment.

Despite those who rail against biblical values, the work of

*Movieguide®* and Christian Film & Television Commission will have a lasting effect on the mass media of entertainment. It has already caused many of those who fashion the popular culture to shift their perspective and reevaluate their relationships. The bottom line is that through this proven strategy, the United States of America may truly become a kinder, gentler nation.

## COMMUNICATE WITH POWER

Another key to winning the culture wars is to equip Christians to produce successful mass media products. Throughout history the church used drama to communicate the gospel. We need to reclaim the power of dramatic communications by producing quality television programs, films, and radio programs. To do so we need to learn and apply the principles of powerful communication.

To produce these good movies and television programs, Christians are going to have to take up scriptwriting and learn that craft much better than the hacks in Hollywood. That means not only learning the principles of powerful communication but also refining the craft, paying one's dues, and going the extra mile.

Christians often want to short-circuit the process of learning how to communicate by appealing to their friends with money on the basis of shared ideological goals. The result is a mediocre, embarrassing film because the scriptwriter, director, or producer has cut short the refinement process necessary to perfecting a script—or they aim the film at their backers instead of at the audience.

## BE APPROVED

The greatest communicators of the gospel of our age have learned the principles of powerful communication. You can do the same. However, it takes work.

The great missionary/explorer Dr. Livingstone left England for Africa at a young age to bring the gospel to the Dark Continent and to deliver the people of Africa from the slave trade. He preached every day for years with little success. He suffered malaria attacks more than sixty times and lost the use of one of his arms to a lion while rescuing a black friend. Then he disappeared into the uncharted jungle.

A brash *New York Herald* reporter named Stanley was sent to find Dr. Livingstone. After one year, by the grace of God, he found Livingstone being cared for by the slave traders he had come to destroy. While on his death bed, Livingstone introduced the reporter to Jesus Christ.

Stanley's articles opened up Africa to the missionaries, and within three years the king of Portugal signed an edict abolishing the slave trade. All Livingstone had set out to do was accomplished, but first he had to become the humble man of character who could serve as a vessel for the pure gospel of Jesus Christ. In a similar manner, you must first submit to God before you can reach the world with the Good News of his salvation. God is more concerned with our character than our accomplishments. He will patiently work on us until we are ready to fulfill the mission he has given us.

## ARE YOU ON GOD'S SIDE?

In the midst of the worst fighting of the Civil War, Abraham Lincoln was approached by a minister, who said, "Mr. President, I hope that the Lord is on your side."

Lincoln replied, "I hope not."

The minister was shocked.

Lincoln explained, "I pray that I am on the Lord's side."

Let us all pray that we are on God's side and that he does his will in and through us to the honor and glory of his holy name.

# FOR MORE INFORMATION
# CALL OR WRITE:

*Movieguide®*
CHRISTIAN FILM & TELEVISION COMMISSION
P.O. Box 190010
Atlanta, GA 31119
(800) 899-6684

## *Movieguide® exists in six formats:*

1. *Movieguide®* TV Program—Featured on E.T.C.: Entertainment That Counts, Paxson Communications, and many other networks and TV stations, *Movieguide®* is broadcast all around the world and in the fifty states. The program is also broadcast on Sky Angel.

3. *Movieguide®* Online—*www.movieguide.org* is available on the Internet, the Worldwide Web.

4. *Movieguide®* Radio Program—The program features capsule summaries and critiques of the latest movies and occasionally news and notes. It is available in two- and five-minute versions. The program is produced every two weeks on CD and mailed to participating radio stations first class and free of charge.

5. *Movieguide®* Early Edition for Publishers—Allows other publications to reprint its reviews in exchange for running a *Movieguide®* advertisement or paying a fee based on the size of readership. This version is produced every two weeks and is now available on the Internet. Those who do not have Internet access can still receive a printed version of our publisher's edition.

6. *Movieguide®: A Family Guide to Movies and Entertainment*— The magazine is published at least every four weeks. Subscription cost is $40 per year (26 issues) or $100 for three years.

# WHAT YOU CAN DO

• Become informed about what is happening in Hollywood and the media by subscribing to *Movieguide®* and other publications that give you information from a biblical perspective.

• Spend your entertainment dollars wisely. Every time you buy a movie ticket, it is a vote to the producer to make more of the same. Cast an informed vote.

• Voice your concerns to those responsible. Write to producers, distributors, and sponsors. The only way they will know your objections is if you tell them. (*Movieguide®* gives you those names and addresses.)

• Actively participate in boycotts and pickets of companies that act contrary to our biblical beliefs.

• Support with your time, talent, and money the ministries and organizations involved in this vital mission field.

• Become a member of Christian Film & Television Commission™ by sending us your name, address, and e-mail address so that we can increase our clout in Hollywood and the mass media.

• Sign the Concerned Americans for Moral Entertainment Pledge and send a copy to:

CONCERNED AMERICANS FOR MORAL ENTERTAINMENT
P.O. Box 190010
Atlanta, GA 31119
(800) 899-6684

# EPILOGUE

Whoever believes in the Son of God has the testimony in himself. Whoever does not believe God has made him a liar, because he has not believed in the testimony that God has borne concerning his Son. And this is the testimony, that God gave us eternal life, and this life is in his Son. Whoever has the Son has life; whoever does not have the Son of God does not have life. (1 John 5:10-12)

# APPENDIX:
# THOUGHTS ON
# JOHN GRANGER'S
## The Hidden Key to Harry Potter

One of the popular new books on Harry Potter is John Granger's *The Hidden Key to Harry Potter*. In this book, Granger contends that Harry Potter is profoundly Christian. Whatever the deficiencies of his assessment in terms of literary criticism and theology, his conclusion may perform an apologetic service by pointing some non-Christians toward the Good News of Jesus Christ. Aside from that, however, his book will only confuse Christians who are not solid in their theology, perhaps leading them into a gnostic maze.

At this point, it should be noted that it is dangerous to get on the wrong side of Mr. Granger. Much of the argument in his book consists of attacks on some brilliant people, such as William Safire and Harold Bloom, on fallacious grounds, after which Mr. Granger relegates them to the dumpster of what he calls "low-road criticism." Apparently "low-road" critics are those who do not agree with him. Unfortunately, he has not provided any critical standards on which to base this assessment.

Mr. Granger's other arguments tend toward the sophomoric, though some ascend to sophistry. Often, though, his conclusions betray a lack of linguistic understanding, which is an interesting problem considering that his brief biography on Amazon.com indicates he may have majored in classical languages.

For example, to claim that Harry Potter is a Christ figure, Granger goes into a sounds-like diatribe that ends with the claim that it would be better to pronounce Harry in the Cockney dialect, as 'Arry, which rhymes with *heir,* and so Harry Potter must be the heir to the throne as Jesus Christ was. This is the same type of reasoning that says forgiveness in the Chinese ideogram is a lamb over a man; therefore, the Chinese must have known about the Lamb of God, Jesus Christ. Of course, this is absurd and would be laughable if there weren't so many people who take such things seriously. Clearly, Mr. Granger is reading into the text rather than allowing the text to speak for itself.

Granger's analysis of the Christian symbolism of the fantasy creatures in Harry Potter is not persuasive. Though there can be Christian allegorical elements in such fantasy animals as the unicorn and the phoenix, Granger needs to show proof within the Potter books that Rowling is using Christian allegory. Granger fails in this regard, unlike the evidence submitted from Tolkien's writings in Bradley Birzer's *J. R. R. Tolkien's Sanctifying Myth*. Rowling herself is coy about the pagan and Christian symbolism that may exist in her book. Thus, although her books do seem to have redemptive motifs in the unicorn and phoenix symbolism, there don't seem to be such redemptive motifs in the other animals Granger mentions. At any rate, the phoenix and hippogriff that appear in the second and third Potter books have their origins in Greek myth, not Christian writings. Furthermore, although www.pantheon.org says that the hippogriff can be a symbol of love, that does not make Rowling's use of the creature a Christian metaphor. In fact, Hagrid says in chapter 6 that the "firs' thing" to know about hippogriffs is that "they're proud" and "easily offended"—not particularly Christian qualities.

Granger ignores the lying and deceit that occur in these books. For example, on page 38 of *Harry Potter and the Prisoner of Azkaban*, we learn that the Minister of Magic has gotten the word of the Prime Minister of England that he won't tell the nonmagical people about the true identity of the escaped murderer Sirius Black, who allegedly murdered thirteen people with a single curse. In fact, the government has also lied to the people that Black is carrying a gun. Later in the book, Hermione tries to deceive Professor Snape in his class by secretly helping Neville Longbottom with a potion. After Snape discovers the ruse, Harry asks Hermione why she didn't lie to Snape and tell him that Neville made the potion all by himself. This is pure moral relativism.

In his book, Granger not only fails to deal with the issue of witchcraft, magical thinking, lying, and rebellion against authority, but he also ignores the prejudice the books seem to show toward nonmagical people, or Muggles. Rowling portrays the Muggles as fools, people who can easily be deceived. Thus, evidence from the Potter books seems to belie Granger's belief that Rowling's books are a treatise against social prejudice. If so, they are a very confused and hypocritical treatise.

Although the books undeniably teach some good moral principles, the series promotes bigotry against Bible-believing Christians opposed to the practice of witchcraft, divination, and necromancy. The Harry Potter books also promote lying, rebellion against authority for self-aggrandizement, and permissiveness toward children who don't obey rules. Finally, these books lead children to accept the idea that they can improve their lives by using magical thinking, witchcraft, and other occult means condemned by the Bible. The publishers of the books and distributors of the movies encourage children who visit their websites to do their own witchcraft spells.

Recently, the High Priest of British White Witches, Kevin Carlyon, credited the popularity of the Harry Potter books with an increased level of paganism and witchcraft in Great Britain. Harry Potter has helped to create "the fastest growing belief system in the world," Carlyon told the Reuters news service on June 19. These books are indeed influencing children, teenagers, and adults to take witchcraft and paganism more seriously.

Mr. Granger contends that the Potter books are popular because they contain Christian themes in them, but he has not proved his case, especially since the books clearly contain elements of witchcraft, divination, necromancy, hypocrisy, bigotry, and moral relativism. Thus, perhaps the books are popular because people are attracted to these sinful elements, not to the positive aspects of the books. Children like to have their wishes fulfilled. The use of witchcraft and magical thinking in the Potter books, as well as some of the humor, seem to fulfill that desire. This desire is not always healthy, however, especially when it leads to a positive attraction to such occult practices as witchcraft and necromancy. Beyond that, the Potter books may also be popular among children because a lot of their action occurs within a school setting, which children of school age can relate to easily. Then, too, the stories focus on a heroic protagonist who faces many tests and other challenges that involve matters of life and death. People respond to stories about heroes.

Granger's arguments serve up a gnostic mix of hidden keys, hidden knowledge, and secret messages. His book resembles the writing of Manley P. Hall, the father of modern occultism, who stretched the truth every which way to build a gnostic, New Age worldview. The only website that shares John Granger's name is pure gnosticism.

The reason that we provide the theological and literary tools in this book is to help readers become adept at discerning the truth and understanding the difference between Christianity and other religions. Clearly, the people who are enamored of Mr. Granger's book do not have the tools to discern the truth.

The Christian story is one of the most universal and appealing because we live in a universe created by God, and God has created a God-shaped vacuum in the human heart. Jesus Christ said that he is the way, the truth, and the life. He offers the free gift of salvation. Having grown up outside of Christianity where works and secret knowledge keep one on the frustrating treadmill of life, I (Ted) find it a wonderful relief to discover the free gift available in Jesus Christ. We hope that Mr. Granger will find that gift, especially since he is an ordained reader in the Orthodox church.

# NOTES

PREFACE: DIVINE ENCOUNTERS AND PARABLES

1. Jim Ware, "'The Lord of the Rings'?! Isn't That a Pretty Pagan Book?" *Wireless Age*, October, November, December, 2001.

## II. SOMETHING ABOUT HARRY

1. Michael D. O'Brien, "Harry Potter and the Paganization of Children's Culture," *Catholic World Report*, Vol. 11, No. 4, April 21, 2001, pp. 52-61.
2. Ibid.
3. Ronald H. Nash, *Christianity and the Hellenistic World* (Grand Rapids: Zondervan, 1984), p. 220.
4. Ibid., pp. 218-219.
5. J. K. Rowling, *Harry Potter and the Prisoner of Azkaban* (New York: Scholastic Inc., 1999), p. 2.
6. Christopher Dawson, *Religion and the Rise of Western Culture* (New York: Image Books, Doubleday, 1957, 1991), p. 27.
7. Ibid., p. 42.
8. Ibid., pp. 53-54.
9. Walter Burkert, *Ancient Mystery Cults* (Cambridge: Harvard University Press, 1987), pp. 51-52.
10. Earle E. Cairns, *Christianity Through the Ages*, rev., enlarged ed. (Grand Rapids: Zondervan, 1981), p. 243.
11. Richard Purtill, *J. R. R. Tolkien: Myth, Morality, and Religion* (San Francisco: Ignatius Press, 1984), p. 4.
12. Ibid.
13. Diane Wiest, "Getting Lost in the Hollywood Matrix," *Tulsa World*, May 24, 2003.
14. Bradley J. Birzer, *J. R. R. Tolkien's Sanctifying Myth: Understanding Middle-Earth* (Wilmington, Del.: ISI Books, 2002), p. 128.
15. J. R. R. Tolkien, *The Fellowship of the Ring*, 2nd ed. (Boston: Houghton Mifflin, 1993), pp. 68-69.
16. O'Brien, "The Paganization of Children's Culture," *Catholic World Report*, pp. 52-61.

## III. THE RING OF TRUTH

1. J. R. R. Tolkien, *The Silmarillion*, 2nd ed., Christopher Tolkien, ed. (New York: Ballantine Books, 2002), pp. 397, 406.
2. Ibid., p. xvii.
3. Ibid., p. 3.

4. J. R. R. Tolkien, *The Lord of the Rings* (Boston: Houghton Mifflin, 1987), p. 322.

## IV. COSMIC BATTLES FOR BEAUTY, VIRTUE, AND HONOR

1. Scholastic Books, "Spellbook," *Karsh's Magick Tips*, www.scholastic.com/titles/twitches/spellbook.htm.

2. Scholastic Books, *Write Your Own Magic Spell*, www.scholastic.com/schoolage/activities/3up/ magicspell.htm.

3. Michael D. O'Brien, "Harry Potter and the Paganization of Children's Culture," *Catholic World Report*, Vol. 11, No. 4, April 21, 2001, pp. 52-61.

4. Ibid.

## V. PILLARS OF MEDIA WISDOM

1. Family Research Council, national public opinion survey, October 1995.

2. According to Nielson Media Research, as reported in the *Los Angeles Times*, August 19, 1995, the average daily television usage in the United States is:

| | | |
|---|---|---|
| Children: | 2-11 | 2 hours, 43 minutes per day |
| Teens: | 12-17 | 2 hours, 52 minutes per day |
| Men: | 18+ | 3 hours, 52 minutes per day |
| Women: | 18+ | 4 hours, 28 minutes per day |
| Daily Home Use: | | 6 hours, 59 minutes per day |

These statistics are significantly lower than the Nielson figures from 1980. Many children, especially in single-family homes and impoverished environments, watch much more television. Assuming that these children are watching whenever the television is turned on, then 30,000 hours is slightly less than six hours a day, excluding two years of infancy and perfunctory days away from the television. According to *U.S. News & World Report*, August 2, 1993, Vol. 115, No. 5, p. 64, "our children watch an astonishing 5,000 hours by the first grade and 19,000 hours by the end of high school—more time than they spend in class."

3. The school time of 11,000 hours assumes four hours per day of classroom time for eight months a year, excluding holidays, from six years old to seventeen years old. Of course, many children start in nursery school, daycare, or preschool, go to after-school programs, and spend much more than four hours per day in the classroom for more than eight months per year. For instance, 16,000 hours assumes six hours a day from age five to seventeen, excluding holidays.

4. Several studies have wired parents and their children with recorders to determine their interaction and have found that parents spend five to fifteen minutes a day with their children. This interaction would total 1,500 hours by the time the child is seventeen.

5. Federal Trade Commission, "Marketing Violent Entertainment to Children," September 2000.

6. See "Joint Statement on the Impact of Entertainment Violence on Children," Congressional Public Health Summit, July 26, 2000, www.aap.org. *Movieguide®* is happy to provide copies of this statement and other articles and position papers.

7. American Psychological Association, 1992 Report: "Big World, Small Screen:

The Role of Television in American Society" (Lincoln: University of Nebraska Press, 1992), quoted by Chicago Associated Press, June 9-11, 1995.

8. See "Joint Statement on the Impact of Entertainment Violence on Children," www.aap.org.

9. abcnews.com, April 9, 2001.

10. Ted Baehr, *The Media-Wise Family* (Colorado Springs: Chariot Victor Publishing, 1998), pp. 87-110. Also, please contact us for articles on the effect of sexual content in the mass media of entertainment.

11. Press release, National Cancer Institute, March 23, 2001.

12. *Los Angeles Times* and *Ventura County Star*, March 29, 2002, citing Peter H. Klopfer, Shameet N. Bakshi, Richard Hockey, Jeffrey G. Johnson, Patricia Cohen, Elizabeth M. Smailes, Stephanie Kasen, and Judith S. Brook, "Kids, TV Viewing, and Aggressive Behavior," *Science*, July 5, 2002; 297: 49-50.

13. Tufts e-news, January 22, 2003.

14. Margaret H. DeFleur and Melvin L. DeFleur, "The Next Generation's Image of Americans: Attitudes and Beliefs Held by Teen-Agers in Twelve Countries: A Preliminary Research Report" (Boston: College of Communication, Boston University, 2003).

15. Ibid.

## VI. CARING IS THE ONLY DARING

1. James Scott Bell is a writer and novelist in Los Angeles. His website is www.jamesscottbell.com. This article originally ran as an op ed piece in the *Los Angeles Times* on October 19, 2002. It is reprinted with the permission of the author.

2. Ibid.

3. Jim Impoco, "TV's Frisky Family Values," *U.S. News & World Report*, April 15, 1996, pp. 58-62.

4. Ibid.

5. Michael Medved, "Hollywood's 3 Big Lies," *Movieguide®*, Vol. 11, No. 01: 960101, reprinted from *Reader's Digest*, October 1995.

6. Teenage Research Institute, Wheaton, Illinois, as reported in *Movieguide®*, Vol. 9, Nos. 3 & 4: 940207.

7. See Jean Piaget, *The Origins of Intelligence in Children*, trans. Margaret Cook (W. W. Norton Co., 1963) and David Elkind, *Children and Adolescents: Interpretive Essays on Jean Piaget* (Oxford: Oxford University Press, 1970).

8. Ted Baehr, *The Media-Wise Family* (Colorado Springs: Chariot Victor Publishing, 1998), pp. 115-117.

9. Which Piaget called the sensorimotor period.

10. Which Piaget called the preoperational period.

11. Barbara J. Wilson, Daniel Lynn, and Barbara Randall, "Applying Social Science Research to Film Ratings: A Shift from Offensiveness to Harmful Effects," *Journal of Broadcasting & Electronic Media*, Vol. 34, No. 4, Fall 1990, pp. 443-468. Reprinted by permission in *Movieguide®*, Vol. 7, No. 14 & 15: 920724.

12. Wilson, et al., *Journal of Broadcasting & Electronic Media*, pp. 443-468, citing C. Hoffner and J. Cantor, "Developmental Differences in Responses to a

Television Character's Appearance and Behavior," *Developmental Psychology* (1985) 21: 1065-1074.

13. Wilson, et al., *Journal of Broadcasting & Electronic Media*, pp. 443-468, citing P. Morison and H. Gardner, "Dragons and Dinosaurs: The Child's Capacity to Differentiate Fantasy from Reality," *Child Development* (1978) 49: 642-648.

14. Wilson, et al., *Journal of Broadcasting & Electronic Media*, pp. 443-468, citing G. G. Sparks, "Developmental Differences in Children's Reports of Fear Induced by Mass Media," *Child Study Journal* (1986) 16: 55-66.

15. Wilson, et al., *Journal of Broadcasting & Electronic Media*, pp. 443-468, citing W. A. Collins, "Interpretation and Inference in Children's Television Viewing." In J. Bryant and D. R. Anderson, eds., *Children's Understanding of Television: Research on Attention and Comprehension* (New York: Academic Press, 1983), pp. 125-150.

16. Wilson, et al., *Journal of Broadcasting & Electronic Media*, pp. 443-468, citing G. Comstock and H. J. Paik, *Television and Children: A Review of Recent Research* (Report No. XX) (Syracuse, N.Y.: Syracuse University, 1987). (ERIC Document Reproduction Service No XX).

17. Wilson, et al., *Journal of Broadcasting & Electronic Media*, pp. 443-468.

18. Ibid., citing A. Bandura, "Influence of Models' Reinforcement Contingencies on the Acquisition of Imitative Responses," *Journal of Personality and Social Psychology*, (1965) 1: 589-595; A. Bandura, D. Ross, and S. A. Ross, "Vicarious Reinforcement and Imitative Learning," *Journal of Abnormal and Social Psychology* (1963) 67: 601-607; M. A. Rosekrans and W. W. Hartup, "Imitative Influences of Consistent and Inconsistent Response Consequences to a Model on Aggressive Behavior In Children," *Journal of Personality and Social Psychology* (1967) 7: 429-434.

19. Wilson, et al., *Journal of Broadcasting & Electronic Media*, pp. 443-468, citing Bandura, "Influence of Models' Reinforcement Contingencies," *Journal of Personality and Social Psychology*, pp. 589-595.

20. Wilson, et al., *Journal of Broadcasting & Electronic Media*, pp. 443-468.

21. Ibid., citing Bandura, "Influence of Models' Reinforcement Contingencies," *Journal of Personality and Social Psychology*, pp. 589-595.

22. Wilson, et al., *Journal of Broadcasting & Electronic Media*, pp. 443-468, citing Collins, "Interpretation and inference." In Bryant and Anderson, eds., *Children's Understanding of Television*, pp. 125-150.

23. Wilson, et al., *Journal of Broadcasting & Electronic Media*, pp. 443-468, citing C. K. Atkin, "Effects of Realistic TV Violence Vs. Fictional Violence on Aggression, *Journalism Quarterly* (1983) 60: 615-621; S. Feshbach, "The Role of Fantasy in the Response to Television, *Journal of Social Issues* (1976) 32: 71-85.

24. Wilson, et al., *Journal of Broadcasting & Electronic Media*, pp. 443-468, citing A. Bandura, *Social Foundations of Thought and Action: A Social Cognitive Theory* (Englewood Cliffs, N.J.: Prentice-Hall, 1986).

25. Wilson, et al., *Journal of Broadcasting & Electronic Media*, pp. 443-468, citing L. R. Huesmann, K. Lagerspetz, and L. D. Eron, "Intervening Variables in the TV Violence-Aggression Relation: Evidence from Two Countries," *Developmental Psychology* (1984) 20: 746-775.

26. Wilson, et al., *Journal of Broadcasting & Electronic Media*, pp. 443-468, citing

Collins, "Interpretation and inference." In Bryant and Anderson, eds., *Children's Understanding of Television*, pp. 125-150.

27. Wilson, et al., *Journal of Broadcasting & Electronic Media*, pp. 443-468, citing L. Berkowitz, "Some Aspects of Observed Aggression," *Journal of Personality and Social Psychology* (1965) 2: 359-369; T. P. Meyer, "Effects of Viewing Justified and Unjustified Real Film Violence on Aggressive Behavior," *Journal of Personality and Social Psychology* (1972) 23: 21-29.

28. Wilson, et al., *Journal of Broadcasting & Electronic Media*, pp. 443-468, citing M. A. Liss, L. C. Reinhardt, and S. Fredrickesen, "TV Heroes: The Impact of Rhetoric and Deeds," *Journal of Applied Developmental Psychology* (1983) 4: 175-187.

29. Wilson, et al., *Journal of Broadcasting & Electronic Media*, pp. 443-468.

30. Ibid., citing Bandura, *Social Foundations of Thought and Action*.

31. Wilson, et al., *Journal of Broadcasting & Electronic Media*, pp. 443-468.

32. Ibid.

33. V. B. Cline, R. G. Croft, and S. Courrier, "Desensitization of Children to Television Violence," *Journal of Personality and Social Psychology* (1973), cited by The UCLA Television Violence Monitoring Report, UCLA Center for Communication Policy, September 1995.

34. William J. Bennett, "Quantifying America's Decline," *Wall Street Journal*, March 15, 1993.

35. Quoted in *Movieguide®*, Vol. 7, No. 3: 920214

36. According to a 1994 UCLA Center for Communication Policy/*U.S. News and World Report* survey mailed to 6,300 decision-makers in the entertainment industry, receiving a 13.76 percent response.

37. See chapter 1.

38. Several studies have been done in this regard, cited earlier in the chapter.

39. *The New York Guardian*, December 1993.

40. *Movieguide®*, Vol. 7, No. 10: 920522

41. John Grisham, "Unnatural Killers," *Movieguide®*, Vol. 11, No. 18: 960826.

42. *Movieguide®*, Vol. 16, No. 10: 010516 and Vol. 16, No. 11: 010530. Michael E. O'Keeffe, Assistant Professor of Religious Studies at Saint Xavier University, teaches a variety of courses in the area of Catholic Studies. He received his doctorate in systematic theology from the University of Notre Dame where he specialized in Christology, Trinitarian theology, and pneumatology. Kathleen Waller is also Associate Professor of Religious Studies at Saint Xavier University. She teaches courses in Christianity and culture, systematic theology, Christian ethics, women's studies, and in the honor's program. A graduate of the University of Chicago Divinity School, Dr. Waller's doctoral dissertation was on the authority of Scripture for Christian theology. Dr. O'Keeffe and Dr. Waller lecture widely on the impact of the mass media on American Christianity and are currently writing a college-level text on religion and film.

43. Paul Tillich, *Christianity and the Encounter of the World Religions* (New York: Columbia University Press, 1963), ch. 1.

44. J. M. Barrie, Kate, in the play *The Twelve-Pound Look* (1910).

45. Gary L. Greenwald, *Seductions Exposed: The Spiritual Dynamics of Relationships* (Santa Ana, Calif. : Eagle's Nest Publications, 1988).

## VII. Once Upon a Time: Worldviews, Fantasy, Myth, and Beyond

1. Dr. Stan Williams, "Popular Motion Pictures Are Imbued with the Center of All Truth," *Catholic Exchange*, www.catholicexchange.com, April 18, 2002.
2. Ibid.
3. Ibid.
4. Ibid.
5. Ibid.
6. Norman Geisler and William D. Watkins, *Worlds Apart: A Handbook of World Views* (Grand Rapids: Baker Book House, 1989), p. 11.
7. Ibid., p. 246.
8. Raymond Chandler, "The Simple Art of Murder: An Essay," *The Simple Art of Murder* (New York: Vintage Books, Random House), p. 18.
9. Thomas Sobchack, "The Adventure Film," in W. D. Gehring, *Handbook of American Film Genres* (Westport: Greenwood Press, 1988), p. 9.

## VIII. The Church, the Media, and the Culture

1. George Barna, Barna Research Group, "Americans Draw Theological Beliefs from Diverse Points of View," *The Barna Update*, October 8, 2002.
2. Ibid.
3. Ibid.
4. Thom S. Rainer, *The Bridger Generation* (Nashville: Broadman and Holman, 1997).
5. Richard H. Niebuhr, *Christ and Culture* (London: Faber and Faber, Ltd., 1952).
6. Joseph E. Coleson, Ph.D., "'To' or 'from'? That Is the Question," *Movieguide®*, Vol. 16, No. 20: 011003.
7. *The Christian World View of Art and Communication* (The Coalition on Revival, Inc., 1986). All rights reserved. The Coalition on Revival, Inc., P. O. Box 1139, Murphys, California 95247.
8. Noam Chomsky, "Politics," in *Language and Responsibility* (New York: Pantheon Books, 1979).
9. In medieval times Christian philosopher William of Occam developed a basic logical principle. The principle states that one should not make more assumptions than the minimum needed. It used to be taught in every science and logic course since it underlies all scientific modeling and theory building. It admonishes us to choose the simplest model from a set of otherwise equivalent models of a given phenomenon.
10. *WorldNetDaily*, June 30, 2002, Compassion Radio, July 8, 2002.
11. John Andrew Murray, "Harry Dilemma," *Movieguide®*, Vol. 15, No. 07: 000417. Murray is the headmaster of St. David's School, Raleigh, N.C., and writer/director of the video *Think About It: Understanding the Impact of TV-Movie Violence*.

## IX. Asking the Right Questions About Frodo and Harry

1. David Outten, "The 21st-Century Pulpit," *Movieguide®*, Vol. 8, No. 12: 930607.
2. William Shakespeare, *Hamlet*, Act 2.

3. See Ted Baehr, "Behind the Myst: An Interview with the Creator of the Most Popular Computer Game," *Movieguide®*, Vol. 11, No. 13: 960617.

4. Samuel Goldwyn was a Hollywood film producer and one of the founders of Metro-Goldwyn-Mayer. His Western Union statement is quoted in the article "Lost in the Cosmos," *Newsweek*, December 10, 1984, p. 94.

5. *USA Today* (August 19, 1996) listed the top grossing movies of all time after adjusting for inflation and found that almost all of them were family movies, mostly G and PG, that had strong moral messages.

6. Lajos Egri, *The Art of Dramatic Writing* (New York: Simon & Schuster, 1960), p. 263.

7. Gerry Mander, *Four Arguments for Elimination of Television* (New York: William Morrow, 1970), pp. 250-254.

8. John 1:14 (KJV).

9. Also note that each medium is composed of one or more tools—from pencil and paper to the sophisticated cameras, recorders, editing machines, satellites, and other hardware and software necessary to produce and broadcast a television program.

10. God's Word is Jesus Christ (John 1). God's Word written is the Bible. The phrase "God's Word written" was used often by the Reformers to emphasize the relation between God the Father, God the Son, and his holy Scripture.

11. Such as Lajos Egri, who wrote the definitive text on scriptwriting, *The Art of Dramatic Writing*. This book is must reading for anyone interested in scriptwriting. *The Art of Dramatic Writing* is the text used at USC, UCLA, and other premiere film and television schools.

12. Timothy Jay, *Cursing in America* (Philadelphia: John Benjamins Publishing Company, 1992).

13. The famous Marxist, Professor Marcuse at the Sorbonne, advocated using language as a weapon. He inspired many of the most renowned Communist revolutionaries in the twentieth century. Even Jane Fonda studied with him.

14. See S. Robert Lichter, Stanley Rothman, and Linda Lichter, *The Media Elite* (Bethesda, Md.: Adler and Adler, 1986). Also see Donald Wildmon, *The Home Invaders* (Wheaton, Ill.: Victor Books, 1985), pp. 18-23 for an excellent analysis of the Lichter-Rothman studies.

15. Lajos Egri, *The Art of Dramatic Writing*, p. 6.

16. Note that movie-maker is being used here to refer to all those people who are responsible for creating a movie, including the screenwriter, the director, the producer, the executive producer, etc.

## X. CONCLUSION: SEEK WISDOM, KNOWLEDGE, AND UNDERSTANDING

1. Recently *Silent Night* has been re-released by a small independent film distributor. It too should be picketed.

# INDEX